10 BASIC SERVANT PRINCIPLES TO IMPROVE LEADERSHIP

Strategies That Highly Effective Leaders Embraced

This book is dedicated to my late father, Chai Va Yang and my mother, Xia Vang. Your hopes and dreams are no longer deferred but realized; I hope you both are proud as you look down on my accomplishments. I love you, always. To my wife, who has always been my inspiration, confidant, and foundation, I love you. And to my children, you are the reason I never stop learning; I am here to hold the ladder for you so you can climb to your full potential. Keep reaching for the unreachable, and never compromise your values.

Table of Contents

Servant leaders are role models. They rise to the challenge and overcome seemingly difficult situations. Anyone who has ever led through challenging times or occupied a leadership role knows it well; leadership is a journey and a process that requires nurture and support (Blanchard, 2019; Greenleaf, 1977; Northouse, 2012; Maxwell, 2007; Spears, 1998). In fact, through nurture and support, most leaders become wiser, more accessible, and more capable (Greenleaf, 1977). The leadership journey is a growth process, and what leaders do and how they lead will either motivate or discourage followers regardless of the organization. Law enforcement is a profession that often demands leaders to make decisions with little to no planning. Thus, autocratic leadership is attractive because it requires controlling subordinates and dictating what they do, often without input or group discussions (Northouse, 2012). Public safety organizations, as a whole, are facing numerous challenges, including but not limited to advancing technologies, recruiting and retention, eroding community trust, misconduct, and low morale, to name a few (Police Chief Magazine, n.d.; Camp et al., 2021). While many police organizations find creative ways to retain and recruit officers by offering incentives such as signing bonuses, step increases, and relocation benefits, police leaders sometimes fail to recognize or develop their most important assets—their current employees.

One of the ways to promulgate trust, build confidence, and inculcate good citizenship is through nurture and support. Servant leadership fosters an environment conducive to growth through a process of nurture and support, thus helping followers mature beyond what was initially thought possible (Blanchard, 2019; Greenleaf, 1977). For instance, supporting employees is as simple as recognizing their contributions to the organization. Recognition and rewards make employees feel valued, which, in turn, motivates them to want to commit to the organization and work harder (Mason, 2016; Wiley, 1993). Servant leadership prioritizes service first, meaning employees are the priority rather than the organization. By shifting the leadership mindset from self-serving to serving others, servant leaders exercise individual consideration and help individuals transcend their self-interest so they can reach their full potential (Blanchard, 2019; Greenleaf, 1977).

The concept of servant leadership may not be foreign to many law enforcement leaders, but the true meaning of servant as a leader seems to elude many officers in leadership positions. While many people have heard of servant-leadership, and some claim to have practiced servant-leadership, few genuinely embody servanthood, which redirects attention from serving the organization to serving individuals (Shim et al., 2016; Greenleaf, 1977). Generally, some people in leadership positions possess traits such as height, looks, confidence, extraversion, and the like, which are commonly espoused as being associated with leadership characteristics (Kirkpatrick & Locke, 1996). Interestingly, Kirkpatrick and Locke posited that certain individuals are born to lead while others are not. However, as Greenleaf (1977) points out, "if the people to lead it well are not there, a better system will not produce a better society" (p. 45). To be sure, Greenleaf asserts that these traits are not guaranteed that the individual will be effective or even good at leading. Some leaders may have leadership characteristics but not possess the skills to lead an organization. This is an empirical fallacy on the part of early researchers; they studied specific traits rather than successful leaders or able servants with the potential to lead (Fleenor, 2006; Greenleaf, 1977).

In modern law enforcement, particularly within the last five to ten years, the vicious recycle of leadership in many police agencies can be characterized as trial and error. Police leaders are being replaced at an unprecedented rate, and to be fair, some moves are influenced by political agenda, while others are due to leadership failure—instances of misconduct, racial injustices, criminal allegations, and more (Li & Mahajan, 2021). Law enforcement executives are being recruited for large and small agencies from the West Coast to the East Coast. For example, a simple internet search for police careers on the International Association of Chiefs of Police (IACP) webpage displays results with dozens of Police Chief positions and a handful of middle management positions available (Jobs, n.d.). The police profession has been tarnished by successions of police misconduct and many questionable encounters with the public, stemming from a police culture that has been unregulated (Armacost, 2004). These negative perceptions, coupled with a struggling economy, have crippled recruitment and retention in law enforcement, destroyed morale, and eroded public trust. A shift in the police paradigm is needed and paramount. I acknowledge the vast pool of leadership concepts, old and new. While there are many leadership styles and practices with various applications—some effective while others not—that are viable options for police leaders, servant leadership is an underutilized concept in law enforcement. Servant leadership is also an understudied leadership concept for scholars; however, servant leadership has gained momentum in many industries as a proven leadership concept in promoting productivity and efficiency (Blanchard, 2019).

This book is based on research of Robert Greenleaf's (1977) servant leadership theory and the ten principles associated with servant leadership—*Listening, Empathy, Healing, Awareness, Persuasion, Conceptualization, Foresight, Stewardship, Commitment to growth,* and *Building Community.* The book unpacks the ten principles of servant leadership, explores each specific characteristic within police agencies, and determines if and how the concept of servant leadership impacts performance and job satisfaction in law enforcement. Servant leadership is not new; however, few scholastic studies on the topic exist, and few studies have comprehensively examined servant leadership in law enforcement. Therefore, servant leadership in law enforcement is an understudied and underutilized body of work and a gap that begs exploration.

PART ONE:
Why Servant Leadership?

America's police chiefs, historically, are white males; according to an online recruitment company, 71 percent of police chiefs are White, 13 percent are Latinos, followed by 8 percent Black and 2 percent Asian (Chiefs of Police., 2022). The disparity of leadership is apparent, and until the leadership pool is more diverse, leadership and the longstanding issues will remain the status quo (Morabito & Shelley, 2015; Yu & Rauhaus, 2019). Morabito and Shelley (2015) suggested that the struggle with recruitment and retention, along with questions of police legitimacy, results from the underrepresentation of women and minorities—this is a leadership issue. There appear to be too few servant leaders who prioritize their people above their own.

Law enforcement in America is very different today than a few decades ago. The concerns have shifted from incarceration to rehabilitation and community building; arrests and incarcerations are no longer the goals of law enforcement. Police leaders across the country today are constantly navigating political challenges, battling internal conflicts, and justifying misconduct while trying to manage and lead organizations (Murray, 2000; Ortmeier & Meese, 2010). This is the result of years of public mistrust and numerous claims of procedural injustices and illegitimacy of police practices (WorkforcesurveyJune2021, n.d.). More recently, many police agencies were forced to undergo massive overhauls due to fatal encounters with individuals of color. According to DeAngelis (2021), there is systemic racism in the police culture. Until diversity improves, the problem will persist because the profession is still primarily dominated by Caucasian males (Bahmani et al., 2021; Morabito & Shelley, 2015). DeAngelis (2021) argues that court decisions and policies contributed to the obscurity of racial injustices; however, a closer look at how policies and decisions are formed points to an institution that lacks leadership and accountability.

Interestingly, according to Enter (2006), only 10% of law enforcement leaders are effective, 80% are ineffective, and 10% are substandard leaders. Many police agencies, as illustrated by the International Association of Chiefs of Police, struggle to fill management positions—particularly Police Chiefs. While some of the issues facing law enforcement today are beyond the control of police leaders, many can be mitigated through servant leadership (Blanchard, 2019; McDevitt, 2009). Effective leadership must start with a solid foundation and clear guiding principles; as Northouse (2012) postulates, leadership is a process, and having a foundation and guiding principles is part of that process. John Maxwell (2007) adds that the leadership process must include bringing someone along, meaning the leader seeks personal and professional growth and coaches and mentors someone on their journey. This leadership conceptualization is scarce in law enforcement, leading to high turnover, low morale, public mistrust, and, worse, misconduct (Badger, 2017; Baker, 2020; Jackson & Lee, 2019).

The preferred leadership model in the military is autocratic (Racaj & Gelev, 2015). Similarly, law enforcement personnel in authoritative positions have a certain influence over their subordinates; for example, they can persuade subordinates to perform certain jobs or task(s) utilizing positional power. Lee (1977) states that "Positional power…derives from the position of a leader in the organizational hierarchy due to ownership and/or appointment or election" (p. 75). As a result, being at the top of the hierarchy in a paramilitary organization becomes attractive. However, Lee (1977), citing the Hawthorne authority-power theory studies, cautioned that the leader's power should incorporate followers' participation. Thus, a downward power flow may not be suitable for organizational change because followers will quickly lose interest without nurture and support, and performances will deteriorate (Blanchard, 2019). Perhaps, more importantly, the concern for followers becomes secondary, and the development of future leaders is viewed as task-oriented rather than a desire. Robert Greenleaf (1977) suggests that the measurement of a good leader is whether the subordinates grow freer, healthier, more autonomous, and are likely to become servant leaders themselves. Servant leaders prioritize service first, putting their interests on hold to focus on others (Greenleaf, 1977). Servant-leaders strive to improve those around them, helping them achieve more than initially thought possible (Greenleaf, 1977); this is precisely the ideal concept for improving leadership.

Nonetheless, the conception of servant leadership in law enforcement has been met with lukewarm welcomes by many, mainly because police leaders, historically, are seen as dynamic and autocratic (Bass, 1985; Burns, 1978; Thomas & Cangemi, 2021). This perception of police leaders is myopic, harmful, and no longer applicable—in most situations—with 21st-century policing. According to former police Chief Joel Shults, who is a contributing writer for *Police1,* the contemporary issues law enforcement faces today, namely civil disobedience, police misconduct, low morale, lack of community support, depleting budget, and recruitment and retention, to name a few, should be of great concern to all leaders or potential leaders intending to manage and lead the new generation of law enforcement (Shults, 2022).

The Purpose of the Study

There is a shortage of officers, and the leadership gap has exacerbated recruitment and retention. The conceptualization of servant leadership is not new. There exists a plethora of scholarly journals on the topic of servant leadership in businesses, higher education, religious institutions, and many other organizations (Amey, 2006; Crowther, 2018; Fry et al., 2007; Khuwaja et al., 2020; Iken, 2005; McGee-Cooper & Looper, 2001). What remains underexplored are the essential principles of servant leadership in law enforcement. There is little empirical evidence connecting servant leaders and law enforcement and whether the leadership style impacts retention and recruitment or increased job satisfaction. In my research, I examined whether there is a correlation between the servant leadership behavior of law enforcement executives and employee job satisfaction in law enforcement.

Servant leadership has been widely studied; however, the studies have also been generalized to all organizations. The old command-and-control leadership style may no longer be suitable for modern law enforcement; instead, a servant leadership paradigm may be necessary to change organizational culture, restore public trust, and improve police-community relationships. As a current law enforcement leader, I acknowledge that leadership in law enforcement is critical for preserving order and maintaining peace in America's communities. Moreover, to this end, leadership style is salient not only for recruiting and retaining police officers but also for improving job satisfaction and developing future leaders. In my research, I performed a quantitative examination to determine whether servant leadership is viable for law enforcement leaders. The research instrument, Organizational Leadership Assessment (OLA), uses a 60-question survey to solicit perceptions of servant leadership with a Likert scale rating of 1, strongly disagree, and 5, strongly agree. The OLA survey was designed to measure organizational health, specifically the Organizational Leadership Assessment (Laub, 1999). Dr. Laub developed the Organizational Leadership Assessment (OLA) to be flexible and suggested that the survey could be used to measure people, a unit, or an entire organization.

Law enforcement is paramilitary and well-known for its autocratic leadership style. Clearly, there is a time and place where autocratic leadership is needed and even desired over all others. Bass (1985) and Burns (1978) suggested that autocratic leaders are favored and highly desired in military and paramilitary organizations because of the authority afforded to the leaders and the control of followers. Furthermore, authors Fiaz et al. (2017) and Rast III et al. (2013) agreed that when decisions must be made, rules and procedures must be followed, and priority is on consistency, autocratic leadership is desired. However, not all situations call for an autocratic leadership response; depending on the circumstance, a softer paternal or servant approach may be more fitting. Greenleaf (1998) and others (Blanchard, 2019; Kouzes & Posner, 2012; Maxwell, 2017) argued that followers must be nurtured and encouraged to grow through modeling, inspiring, and engaging consistently. Two law enforcement agencies, one from the Midwest and a second from the Southwest of the United States, were surveyed. The smaller agency employed 76 sworn officers, and the larger agency employed 1,184 sworn officers. The study aimed to examine if there are correlations between servant leadership, job satisfaction, and agency size and whether there is a difference in perceptions between servant leadership and job satisfaction based on years of service and levels of education.

Significance of the Study

Robert Greenleaf popularized servant leadership in the 1970s. Other researchers and practitioners (Blanchard, 2019; Russell, 2010; Sendjaya & Sarros, 2002; Spears, 2010) have since contributed empirical data to the saliency of servant leadership. The studies of servant leadership and its impact on organizational leaders are gaining popularity. However, Koehler and Pankowski (1997) suggested that many empirical studies lump leadership studies into one group—a one-size-fits-all. As law enforcement agencies nationwide struggle with recruitment and retention, low morale, public mistrust, and rising crime, police leaders most open to reform are the ones leaving the profession. Consequently, at a time when leaders must rise to the challenge, it appears that Police Chiefs and elected Sheriffs are either resigning, retiring, or being terminated at an unprecedented rate, more than in years past (Morin, 2017). Moreover, according to a report in "The Marshall Project," police executives are not the only ones leaving the profession in droves;

but civilians and sworn officers, from line supervisors down to patrol officers, are calling it quits (Duret & Li, 2023; Greenblatt, 2020).

According to the Police Executive Research Forum, a non-profit group that conducts policy research and management services to support law enforcement, the number of officers resigning increased by 18 percent in 2020-21 as compared to 2019-20, and the number of retirements jumped to 45 percent during the same period (Workforce survey2021, n.d.). The climate between the public and law enforcement in the last five years—George Floyd, racial injustice, police reform, and COVID-19—has contributed to the dire situation law enforcement faces today. Aside from job satisfaction, the driving force behind the exodus ranges from public scrutiny to unrealistic government expectations to media scrutinization and lack of confidence from those being led. Leaders of the profession must be willing to self-reflect and answer the following question: Why are people leaving?

Effective leadership is needed in every organization if the desire is to grow and become successful. Leaders enable organizations to become profitable and prosper; to this end, leadership styles and the environment in which followers operate dictate whether a company succeeds or fails (Blanchard, 2019; Fiaz et al., 2017; Kotter, 2012). From a historical perspective, law enforcement is a profession where command-and-control leadership is preferred over all others. However, in recent times, this noble profession has come under heavy public scrutiny for misconduct leading to civil unrest and other anti-police sentiments, and the byproduct negatively impacts morale, job satisfaction, recruitment, and retention. To exacerbate the situation, police executives are leaving the profession at an alarming rate, leaving a significant leadership gap in what was once a highly sought-after position—Police Chiefs (McGinty, n.d.). Equally alarming is the rate at which officers leave the profession and the inability of police departments to fill those vacancies. The issue extends beyond public demands of transparency and accountability.

In a Harvard Business Review article, authors Gibson, O'Leary, and Weintraub (2020) suggested that employees, officers, and civilians want to work in an environment where they are valued and appreciated. This observation is not only accurate but factual. In my thirty years of police service with one agency, I will admit that change is foreign to many organizational leaders; some leaders find reasons to resist or accept changes. As a middle manager, I concede that it was challenging to institute organizational change; however, I believe that small incremental changes can cascade up and down the organization, impacting future changes. My research on servant leadership led to the four research questions that guided this research as follows:

Research Questions

1. To what extent do characteristics of the six subscales of servant leadership behavior (*values people, develops people, builds community, displays authenticity, provides leadership, shares leadership*) correlate with the perceptions of police officers or deputy sheriffs regarding job satisfaction?

2. Is there a correlation between servant leadership and employee job satisfaction based on the agency size: (a) 50 or more officers or deputies but less than 500 and (b) 500 or more officers or deputies?

3. Is there a difference in how officers perceive job satisfaction based on their years of service?

4. Is there a difference in how officers perceive job satisfaction based on their levels of education?

Theoretical Framework

Servant leadership is a pragmatic leadership concept that has gained considerable momentum as a preferred leadership style to foster organizational change by improving employee performance. The theoretical framework of servant leadership is whether the people being served grow as individuals. Robert Greenleaf (1977, as cited in Burkhardt & Joslin, 2020) suggested that a person's growth is determined by whether they become "healthier, wiser, freer, and [*sic*] more autonomous" (p. 5) or, at the very least not further deprived. While servant leadership dates back to the biblical era—the teachings from Christianity—it was Robert Greenleaf (1977) who conceptualized the leadership theory in the 1970s. Greenleaf (1977) believes leaders must desire to serve before consciously choosing to lead. Greenleaf contends that this manifestation leads to the assurance that followers' priorities come first. Implementing servant leadership in the private sector has been shown to increase work productivity, efficiency, job satisfaction, boost morale, and improve organizations (Allen et al., 2018; Charles, 2015; Craun & Henson, 2022; Ebener, 2011; Ebener & O'Connell, 2010). Moreover, Spears (1996) added that individuals and institutions had adopted servant leadership as either a personal or corporate philosophy. However, the study of servant leadership and its impact on law enforcement is limited and necessitates attention.

The primary objective is to examine whether there are correlations between servant leadership and job satisfaction and whether servant leadership is a viable option for law enforcement. Guided by the four aforementioned questions, the study examined to what extent servant-leadership characteristics influence the perceptions of line-level supervisors and police officers in the police department based on the six subscales (*values people, develops people, builds community, displays authenticity, provides leadership, shares leadership*) of the Organizational Leadership Assessment (OLA) instrument (Laub, 1999). Next, the research explored whether there are correlations between servant leadership and employee job satisfaction based on the agency's size. The tertiary objective is to determine whether differences exist in officers' perceptions of servant leadership based on demographics (tenure and education levels). Servant leaders choose to serve first and are good stewards of followers and the organizations (Greenleaf, 1977; Sendjaya & Sarros, 2002). The concept of servant leadership is the opposite of autocratic leadership and slightly different from transformational leadership; it represents a shift from the command-and-control leadership concept, which has been pervasively practiced throughout law enforcement communities in America. Leadership is challenging. There is no question about it. Being a servant leader will require courage because you challenge the status quo and accept leadership transformation.

PART TWO:
The Principles of Servant Leadership

Robert Greenleaf (1977) envisioned servant leadership as pragmatic, genuine, and enriching. His written work, *Servant Leadership: A Journey into the Natures of Legitimate Power and Greatness*, compiled a series of essays he produced on servant leadership as a senior executive at AT&T and later as an influential leadership consultant. From the series of essays Greenleaf wrote, many themes and characteristics emerged as fundamental principles of servant leaders. More specifically, in *The Servant as Leader*, Greenleaf wrote extensively on key principles of servant leaders. According to Spears (1998), the core characteristics of servant leadership are as follows: The first principle is *listening*. The act of listening first when responding to a problem allows leaders to understand the goals and aspirations of followers. Here is what happens when leaders genuinely listen. They hear emotions with vocals and see excitement, happiness, or distress; thus, the leader can better serve and help individuals transcend what was initially thought possible. Greenleaf (1977) asserts that "a true natural servant automatically responds to any problem by listening *first*" (p. 17). The second is *acceptance and empathy*. Accepting an individual's imperfection and being able to work with a variety of talents is the mark of a great leader. Servant leaders empathize with others; they know of human imperfection and always empathize, never reject (Greenleaf, 1977). This principle speaks to a leader's ability to be open-minded. A leader who can envision himself in another's predicament will be more likely to empathize and accept those he leads.

The third characteristic or principle is *healing*; wellness is a concern for followers and leaders (Greenleaf, 1977). People come from all walks of life, and everyone has unique needs and challenges, whether emotionally or spiritually. Wellness is the new norm for law enforcement agencies nationwide, and the shift in police culture makes healing a focal point. For instance, in the 1970s, 1980s, and 1990s, it was considered a weakness if someone sought counseling or, worse, that individual officer was ostracized. Blanchard (2019), Greenleaf (1977), and Spears (2010) suggested that self-healing and making "Whole" of those being led strengthens the relationships between leaders and followers; therefore, servant leaders take advantage of the opportunity to comfort those they encounter. Greenleaf (1977, p. 36) contends that "the servant-leader might also acknowledge that his own healing is his motivation, [*and*] the search for wholeness is something they share." Self-healing then leads to *Awareness*—the fourth principle. Self-awareness is being grounded and understanding one's strengths and weaknesses. Awareness also means having broad perspectives so that leadership opportunities are not missed. Greenleaf (1977) observes that awareness is "value building and value clarifying, and it armors one to meet the stress of life by helping build serenity in the face of stress and uncertainty" (p. 27). The fifth principle of servant leadership is *Persuasion*. Servant leaders must be convincing without coercion and be persistent but gentle when seeking compliance (Greenleaf, 1977). Persistent persuasion over positional coercion is how servant leaders build relationships, trust, and respect.

The sixth servant leadership principle is *Conceptualization*. Good leaders consistently learn and grow; rather than identifying more problems, they conceptualize futuristic opportunities and solutions. This characteristic is salient in creating a vision and transforming individuals and organizations. A leader who can conceptualize beyond the day-to-day operation will enrich the lives of followers and transform organizations beyond what was initially thought possible (Greenleaf, 1977; Spears, 1998). Conceptualization leads to the seventh principle—*Foresight*. The two characteristics are similar, but foresight is being able to see farther, sooner, and before others. This is not a psychic ability, but rather, in this context, it is about learning from the past, dealing with the present, and projecting the future (Spears, 1998). Greenleaf (1977) states, "Foresight means regarding the events of the instant moment and constantly comparing them with series of projections made in the past and at the same time projecting future events" (p. 25-26).

Stewardship is the eighth principle. Servant leaders are good stewards to those they lead; they advocate, assume responsibility, and are committed to serving others (Block, 2013; Spears, 1998). To be clear, this is different from over-identifying with subordinates to the point where the leader neglects his commitment to the organization—his duties. Greenleaf (1977) explains that servant-leaders care deeply, not only about the individuals but also about the organization. It is a balancing act; Greenleaf sees stewardship as trustees of the organization and asserts that stewards care for the institution, "which means that they care for all of the people the institution touches" (p. 55). The penultimate principle is the *Commitment to the growth of others* (Greenleaf, 1977).

Greenleaf proposed that servant leaders prioritize serving first; thus, they are committed to the growth of those in their organization. The commitment to the growth of those you lead is more than providing opportunities; it requires the leader to hold the ladder so those being led can climb to their full potential. Blanchard (2019) adds that commitment to growing others allows servant leaders to build lasting, sustainable relationships. Servant leaders understand productive and efficient employees' impact on the organization when they help followers transcend their self-interest and reach their full potential (Greenleaf, 1977; Spears, 1998). The tenth principle is *Building community* (Greenleaf, 1977). There is a detachment as society advances from local communities to industrialized institutions regarding servant leadership. Greenleaf argues that those being served should be loved, which requires a community—team environment. Relationships, trust, and respect are unlimited in a community or a team (Blanchard, 2019; Kotter, 2012; Maxwell, 2007). However, "Where there is not a community, trust, respect, and ethical behavior are difficult for the young to learn and the old to maintain" (Greenleaf, 1977, pp. 38-39). Building community is essential, whether inside the organization or in an actual community.

Servant leadership, while similar to transformational leadership, is different in that the focus or priority is on enriching the lives of those being led. Transformational leadership, on the other hand, focuses on ensuring the organization succeeds by improving both the leader and subordinate (Burns, 1978). Servant leaders focus on serving first to ensure followers become healthier, more intellectually advanced, autonomous, less dependent, and inspired to become leaders themselves (Greenleaf, 1977; Heyler & Martin, 2018). In contrast, transformational leaders focus on leading and influencing individuals to achieve higher than initially thought possible. Ironically, law enforcement exists to provide service to people through serving and protecting, and servant leadership lays the foundation for both leaders and followers. When leaders practice the ten core principles of servant leadership, followers are encouraged to emulate and pass on servant gratitude to community members. Greenleaf (1977) asserts eloquently, "All that is needed to rebuild community as a viable life form for large numbers of people is for enough servant-leaders to show the way" (p. 39). As numerous authors assert, if law enforcement is to change, it must be from within, starting with servant leaders showing the way.

Servant leadership is a paradigm shift from the command-and-control concept law enforcement leaders historically embraced. The diversity that makes up today's police force, although not yet considered equitable representation, has made tremendous progress, according to the PEW Research Center. The PEW Research Center is a nationally recognized nonpartisan research organization that conducts research to inform and shape public opinions (Dimock, 2010). According to data from PEW and the Bureau of Justice Statistics, women in law enforcement make up twelve percent of full-time sworn officers, an increase from 8 percent in 1987, and twenty-seven percent were racial and ethnic minorities, an increase of nearly one hundred and fifty percent (Mitchell, 2017; Reaves, 2015). Today, there are more women and minorities in law enforcement than in years past (Reaves, 2015). Also, a study on the working-age population in the U.S. indicates that the workforce is younger than in years past. Therefore, leadership is extremely salient in recruitment and retention, building relationships, improving performance, and increasing job satisfaction (Zane, 2023).

In the last several decades, leadership studies have intrigued scholars in various fields, from private industries to nonprofits to religious groups to government entities (Allen et al., 2018; Amey, 2006; Bass, 1990; Bass & Avolio, 1990; Burns, 1978; Sendjaya, 2005; Yang et al., 2021). Some typical leadership styles of law enforcement leaders are autocratic, transactional, democratic, and transformational. When decisions must be made, rules and procedures must be followed, and priority is on consistency, autocratic leadership is highly desired; however, this leadership concept is not sustainable (Van Vugt et al., 2004). Transactional leadership, on the one hand, is contingent on an exchange where followers are rewarded for good performances (Bass, 1990). Democratic leadership, on the other hand, assumes a democratic process where leaders and followers make decisions together or, at the very least, have the opportunity to express opinions (Hendriks & Karsten, 2014). Nevertheless, transformational leadership suggests leaders elevate followers by raising their awareness so followers may achieve more than initially thought possible (Bass, 1990). Change is often necessary to move leadership forward regardless of the success of tried and true leadership concepts. Law enforcement in America has come under fire for many reasons—namely, public mistrust, acts of misconduct, and rising crime resulting in the mass exodus of officers and supervisors.

The study aims to investigate whether servant leadership is applicable in law enforcement. In applying the theory of servant leadership, the study hopes to answer (1) To what extent do characteristics of the six subscales of servant leadership behavior (values people, develops people, builds community, displays authenticity, provides leadership, shares leadership) correlate with the perceptions of police officers or deputy sheriffs regarding job satisfaction?, (2) Is there a correlation between servant leadership and employee job satisfaction based on the agency size (a) 50 or more and (b) 500 or more officers or deputies?, (3) Is there a difference in how officers' perceive job satisfaction based on the years of service?, and (4) Is there a difference in how officers' perceive job satisfaction based on the levels of education?

Servant leadership is an understudied concept in law enforcement. This scholastic research challenges the status quo and adds the law enforcement workforce to the many organizations to explore servant leadership. Prior servant-leadership studies have uncovered organizational improvements and proficiencies, from higher education to business corporations to religious institutions, to name a few (Aboramadan et al., 2020; Liden et al., 2014; Melinda & Antonio, 2019). This research explores servant leadership in a culture dominated mainly by autocratic leadership. This research explores whether servant leadership can change law enforcement leaders' behaviors and attitudes, which may inspire followers and ultimately improve organizational performance.

Limitations of the Study

As with the majority of studies, there are limitations associated with this quantitative research. Therefore, the results must be interpreted with caution, and researchers should be mindful of the number of constraints. First, the sample population only comes from two law enforcement agencies, one from the Midwest and the other from the Southwest of the United States. Second, only agencies with a minimum of 50 or more sworn officers or deputies were considered for this study. According to the U.S. Department of Justice, Bureau of Justice Statistics, there are about 18,000 law enforcement agencies in the U.S., including federal, state, county, and municipal agencies (Banks et al., 2016). Moreover, by excluding law enforcement agencies with fewer than 50 officers or deputies, the study is biased towards micro agencies that are culturally homogeneous. The third concern is that researchers may find it difficult to replicate using the same sample population due to limited access granted to the public and the hesitancy of police leaders to entertain such research studies. The fourth limitation is whether current leaders support research efforts. Fifth, servant leadership is an emerging concept for law enforcement; therefore, subjectivity is expected to impact the outcome. The sixth limitation concerns the geographical region where the sample population was drawn, which may influence the level of responses depending on culture, training, and leadership influence. Researchers should bear in mind the aforementioned limitations; in some instances, the listed limitations may not be the case for this or other studies.

The study contains delimitation by focusing only on municipal and county law enforcement agencies and excluding departments with fewer than 50 sworn officers or deputies. This narrow scope of study may create a bias toward police leaders in small agencies and those at the state and federal levels who may embrace the concept of servant leadership. However, focusing on municipal and county agencies with 50 or more sworn officers encompasses the country's two most common law enforcement organizations, and the findings are most likely to apply to general law enforcement. Law enforcement agencies are different throughout the United States; aside from the branches of service—federal, state, county, and local agencies—law enforcement differs from state to state and city to city. For example, some states require officers to wear a body-worn camera while working in a uniform capacity, whereas others are just now exploring the option. Furthermore, smaller agencies tend to be more homogeneous—single-race dominated—thus preventing diverse perspectives. Finally, while access to the same population may be limited, future studies should consider expanding the research to include smaller law enforcement agencies and departments from other geographical regions of the United States, including state and federal agencies.

Assumptions

Several assumptions underlie this study. First, the study assumes that the selected population will, to the best of their ability, report leadership characteristics that reflect behaviors indicative of servant leaders. Second, the instrument used to predict servant leadership characteristics is deemed reliable and valid for measuring leadership characteristics in law enforcement. Third, leadership characteristics measured by the instrument reflect supervisors from the rank of lieutenants and higher. Fourth, the agencies studied value leadership development and are able to contribute meaningful views. Fifth, the views of the respondents are deemed honest and truthful. Sixth, servant leadership characteristics are prevalent only with limited law enforcement leaders.

PART THREE:
The Foundation of Servant Leadership

In my research, I examined existing scholarships on servant leadership and its impact on scholars and organizations. It was clear to me that the popularity of servant leadership continues to positively impact industrial performances, employee engagement, and job satisfaction. As a life-long leadership student, I was intrigued by the servant leadership principles and curious about how servant leadership characteristics impact perceived job satisfaction in law enforcement. The discussion on the collage of servant-leadership comes from various industries, from business to higher education, religious groups, and government entities, which have experienced improved employee performances and job satisfaction.

Law enforcement has experienced significant setbacks in the last decade due to a myriad of issues, from rising crime to rapid changes in federal, state, and local statutes, to recruiting and retention, to low morale, to name a few. The aforementioned suggested that a paradigm shift in leadership style may be necessary. While limited scholastic research exists between servant leadership and perceived job satisfaction in law enforcement, my research draws from closely related research studies, and the collage of existing literature serves as a model for this book. Law enforcement leaders, historically, are dynamic and autocratic in nature. This leadership style is part of the issues that have exacerbated the many challenges law enforcement faces today.

Leadership, in general, is the process of influence, which means being responsible for the development and growth of followers (Northouse, 2012). However, the lack of consistency in defining leadership and the diverse perspectives have proved challenging for many organizations to subscribe to one or more leadership styles. Servant leadership promulgates trust and community building to improve individuals by helping followers achieve more than initially thought possible (Greenleaf, 1977; Miao et al., 2014a). Robert Greenleaf suggests that this leadership process focuses on and ensures that followers fulfill their potential. The divergence from law enforcement leaders' dynamic and authoritarian leadership styles may be necessary to improve performance and increase job satisfaction.

There is a consensus among scholars that leaders' behavior influences followers, and when leaders show empathy, engage in shared values and beliefs, and foster relationships (commit to the growth of others), followers become more engaged, productive, and satisfied. Whereas when a leader seeks title and power, little care and attention are devoted to followers, which leads to fear, low morale, poor performances, and ultimately, poor service. Servant leadership is not an emerging concept; however, few studies have comprehensively examined servant leadership in law enforcement. Thus, it is an understudied body of work and a gap that cannot be ignored. This research fills the gap by exploring the relationship between employee perceptions of servant leadership and how employee perceptions of the six constructs of servant leadership impact job satisfaction in law enforcement.

The research commences with examining seminal works by Robert Greenleaf—books and journal articles—to set the foundation and expand general knowledge on the construct of servant-leadership. The review then broadened to include published literature, peer-reviewed journals, and quantitative studies. In this section, my research reviews and integrates what other scholars have done and written on servant leadership in businesses, educational institutions, government, and religious organizations and the impact servant leadership has on people and organizations. The research concludes with contrasting perspectives where critiques of servant leadership were uncovered, discussed, and acknowledged.

Finally, while servant leadership has been extensively studied and practiced, what remains elusive is servant leadership in law enforcement. This research adds to existing studies by exploring servant leadership principles in law enforcement and whether servant leadership plays a role in improving officers' performances and job satisfaction as with other industries. Future servant leadership studies are encouraged to explore paramilitary organizations, namely law enforcement.

Foundation of Servant Leadership

The Servant as Leader

The foundation for this research comes from Greenleaf's (1977) book, "*Servant Leadership: A Journey into the Nature of Legitimate Power and Greatness*," a compilation of several of Greenleaf's essays on servant leadership. This book consisted of multiple essays Greenleaf wrote over several years, in which he discussed the foundation of servant leadership and the application of servant leadership in business, education, and religious institutions. The first essay, "*The Servant as Leader*," was written out of concern for the lack of leadership in higher education institutions, which Greenleaf referred to as a "crisis of leadership" (p. 4). Greenleaf referred to this crisis as the unwillingness of educators to recognize and give credibility to servant leadership as they do with doctors, lawyers, teachers, and other professions. At this very junction, I found Greenleaf's view fascinating; the "unwillingness" of some law enforcement leaders to accept change and the crisis our profession faces today are indicative of his views. Two other essays followed: *The Institution as Servant* and *Trustees as Servants*. In the former, Greenleaf addresses the capacity to serve, and the latter refers to being a servant of a governing board of an institution. Greenleaf (1977) proposed that a leader must first have the desire to serve, followed by a conscious decision to lead; thus, the leader is a servant first. Clearly, most, if not all, law enforcement individuals enter this profession with a desire to serve or to do good. Having spent three decades as a law enforcement professional, I do not believe anyone signed on to this profession with evil intentions.

In his first essay, the conceptualization of *servant as leader* [emphasis] was inspired by Hermann Hesse's *The Journey to the East* (Greenleaf, 1977). *The Journey to the East* is a story about a humble covert leader serving a group of travelers as their servant. The story's main character is Leo; Leo is a servant who joined a group of men on a mythical journey. Leo sustains the group by performing menial chores and lifting their spirits until, one day, he becomes missing and sends the group into disarray, eventually abandoning the journey. Years later, one of the travelers finds Leo and takes him to the Spiritual Order that organized the journey. There, the man learned that Leo, who he thought was a servant, was the Order's leader and the highest-ranking Orderly. The servant parable in *The Journey to the East* suggests that a leader is humble and primarily responsible for serving first (Greenleaf, 1977).

In "*The Servant as Leader*," Greenleaf addressed the question of "who is the servant-leader?" He suggested that a servant-leader genuinely desires to serve and prioritizes serving others before self; Greenleaf (1977) contends that it is a conscious desire and a preference of the heart. He conceptualizes that the leader is first a servant, and he argues that this perception is different from someone who desires positional power, authority, or title—the leader-first mentality. The latter promulgates self-interest, whereas the former emphasizes service to others. To support the conceptualization of *servant as leader*, Greenleaf (1977) identified ten characteristics or principles of servant-leadership in his first essay. The servant leadership characteristics and principles are explained as follows:

The first attribute is *listening and understanding*. This first attribute is listed in many scholastic works as *listening*. However, Greenleaf's original work suggested that listening and understanding are necessary skills for effective, open communication. According to Greenleaf (1977), servant-leaders listen as their first course of action in any interaction.

The second attribute is *acceptance and empathy*. Acceptance and empathy complement each other, and both require being open without reservations. The willingness to project one's consciousness onto others, meaning seeing the view from another's perspective, is a critical element of acceptance and empathy. Greenleaf (1977) asserts that this is how trust is established and sustained. *Foresight* is the third attribute. Greenleaf agrees that leading is difficult, but a leader must have the ability to see farther, sooner, and clearer than those they lead. He suggests that whether it is an intuition based on training and experience or just gut feeling, a leader must have "a sense for the unknowable and be able to foresee the unforeseeable" (Greenleaf, 1977, p. 22).

The fourth attribute of a servant-leader is *awareness and perception*. Greenleaf (1977) argues that servant-leaders must be self-aware to expand depth perception, and awareness allows for information to flow freely without intense scrutiny because of confidence in one's alertness. Without awareness and depth perception, leadership opportunities are missed, coaching moments are overlooked, and relationships are lost.

Next, a servant-leader must be persuasive; thus, *persuasion* is the fifth attribute. Leaders have influence, good or bad, and whether the sphere of influence is large or small, the power to influence has great implications. Greenleaf (1977) professed that to persuade others, one must do as John Woolman did, one at a time with "gentle but clear and persistent persuasion" (p. 29). John Woolman was a Quaker farmer who preached the Quaker doctrine. In serving others, Greenleaf professed, persuasion can be achieved through gratitude and reciprocation; however, the servant-leader must initiate the process, not the other way around—servant first.

Conceptualization is the sixth attribute of servant leadership. Greenleaf (1977) states, "The spirit (not knowledge) is power" (p. 33). He explains that a vision creates a timeline that dictates when a project starts and has a prediction for future outcomes. Moreover, a clear vision encompasses goal setting that supports organizational commitments. Servant leaders conceptualize a future with not only organizational growth but also the growth of followers.

Greenleaf (1977) professed that a servant leader's seventh attribute is *healing and serving.* He explains that a servant-leader seeks to complete or make whole through inspiration and motivation. Greenleaf suggested that the search for wholeness is a shared desire of the servant-leader and those being led because servant-leaders want those they serve to be well mentally and spiritually. Now, more than ever, law enforcement must embrace wellness, mentally and spiritually. My experience is that when officers and professional staff are well mentally and spiritually, they perform better and are more efficient. The by-product is an improved organization.

The eighth attribute of a servant leader is *community*, and the goal of *community* is collaboration and teamwork. According to Greenleaf (1977), in society's rapid advancement, the development of institutions has done more harm than good, and it limits the liability of servant leaders. In defining community, Greenleaf suggests that it would be challenging to build trust, respect, and ethical behavior for young people without a sense of community. Teamwork is essential in law enforcement; we routinely operate in a team environment, particularly in large departments where resources are allowed.

Servant-leaders are committed to the growth and well-being of followers; thus, the ninth attribute is a c*ommitment to the growth of people.* Greenleaf (1977) postulates that servant-leaders put people first, meaning that leaders must ensure followers have opportunities to grow and reach their full potential within the institution. He further explains that institutions that use people for short-term gain will not see long-term achievement versus those that put people first. In leadership development, this is one of the most valuable attributes of a leader, coach, or mentor. We will not develop more leaders if we are not committed to developing others.

The tenth attribute is *stewardship.* Greenleaf (1977) explains that organizational stewards see the big picture and are not only good stewards of followers but also the caretakers of the whole institution. In the context of servant-leadership, steward means acting on behalf of others or organizations. Greenleaf went on to say that institutional stewards have obligations to ensure the group shares a common purpose by acting as servant first, a distinct contrast from one who is leader first. This ideology of institutional steward led to the writing of *The Institution as Servant.*

The Institution as Servant

The second essay Greenleaf (1977) discussed on servant-leadership was based on his personal experiences with institutions such as churches, universities, and businesses—The Institution as Servant. Greenleaf suggested that major institutions (or those leading the institution) should build a better society by serving and providing opportunities to its people. This action, Greenleaf described as *trustee,* represents the governing boards of institutions, and the *trustees should* ensure institutions move towards a distinction as servants. Greenleaf made the following observations on numerous industry performances: he shared that government agencies rely too much on coercion and not enough on persuasion; businesses are too dependent on past performances; healthcare services are inadequate; universities are not equipped to handle modern pedagogy; and churches serve to alienate. In sum, Greenleaf suggests that while various institutions are declining, *trustees* hold the key to improving institutions because they care for the institution and the people who serve the institution.

Trustees as Servant

In *Trustees as Servant,* Greenleaf (1977) argues that leaders of institutions (Trustees) must act on behalf of the people in the institutions. He provided distinctions between trustees, management, and leadership; trustees hold the public's trust, whereas management dictates trustees' action, and leadership is reserved for individuals with the competency to lead an institution. Greenleaf suggested that many institutional trustees served to satisfy legal requirements merely and under cover of legitimacy rather than as servants, and such trustees do more to create mistrust than having no trustees.

Greenleaf (1977) contends that trustees must include multiple views that complement one another to create a better society. Moreover, trustees should be independent of the institutions to avoid improprieties. Trustees are the builders of trust when administrators fail, and where inadequacy prevails, it is the responsibility of trustees to replace it with someone who has the ability and devotion to lead. Therefore, trustees must choose to be servants, and these servants must understand their roles—set goals, appoint executives, assess institutional performances, and take action. Greenleaf concludes that to build a trusted society, senior executives must set aside pride and be ready and willing to learn from young, able people to ensure that institutions perform at their optimum.

Joseph and Winston (2005) conducted a correlational study on leadership and organizational trust and found that businesses that adopted the servant-leadership model had higher trust among leaders and the organization. The study corroborated the servant leadership theory; succinctly, when followers trust in leaders, organizational trust and productivity become the by-product. Along the same lines, Eva et al. (2018) found a correlation between servant leadership and organizational performance. For example, when leaders invest in followers, their action ignites followers' desire to reciprocate, which leads to higher performances. This means that where there is trust and autonomy, there is improvement in performance, efficiency, and productivity.

Servant Leadership in Business Organizations

In his book, "*Leading at a Higher Level*," Blanchard (2019) proposed the concept of leadership as an inverted pyramid with the tip pointing at the bottom and the flat base at the top. The inverted pyramid is the foundation of servant leadership—leadership power that emanates from a desire to serve rather than positional power or rank. The inverted pyramid concept is that leaders exist to serve, promote followers, and propel them to a higher status; hence, leaders are at the bottom of the pyramid. Blanchard (2019) explained it pragmatically. He suggests servant leadership has two parts: *servant* and *leader* [emphasis]. In reverse order, Blanchard notes that a *leader* is responsible for the vision and direction, whereas implementing the vision refers to the *servant* aspect. Blanchard posits that it is the leader's responsibility, as stewards of the institution, to communicate the vision of what the organization stands for and how to get there. This proactive role, explained Blanchard, is the servant aspect of servant leadership, and many organizations fail because they do not prioritize service first.

In *Leadership is an Art*, DePree (1989) suggests that leading has three components: first, define reality; second, be a servant; and third, express gratitude. The concept of servant leadership is not new, and many organizations have leveraged its effectiveness. For instance, Max DePree, former CEO of Herman Miller Furniture Company, posits that the arabesque relationship between life experience and job knowledge must be integrated for a positive outcome (Ladkin & Taylor, 2010). Furthermore, DePree (2002) declares that his company became successful by listening, ensuring employee autonomy, and modeling the way, a servant-first practice as Greenleaf (1977) had imagined. DePree was a proponent of servant leadership and contributed substantially to the practice of servanthood. He argues that the primary responsibility of a leader in any organization is to help others reach their full potential through mentoring. Similar to the wisdom of Greenleaf,

DePree agrees that the most rewarding feeling is watching the maturation of those served become leaders themselves.

Max DePree (1989) acknowledges the saliency of building and nurturing relationships—Greenleaf's community-building principle. In *Leadership is an Art,* DePree (1989) shared his views and affirmation on community building; he argues that relationships are at the heart of community building. Two of Greenleaf's servant leadership principles—a commitment to growth and building community—are discussed in Leadership *is an Art.* DePree posits that society lives and works in interdependent groups, and relationship competency improves human connections. Human connection is part of building community, and by connection, individuals are impacted by diverse skills that allow them to reach their full potential through the community. In his writing, DePree states, "Only in communities can we grow and prosper as persons and reach our potential" (p. xi). Building community—servant leadership—is not limited to business corporations but is also fitting for education institutions, religious organizations, or government agencies.

In *The Essentials of Servant-Leadership: Principles in Practice*, Mcgee-cooper et al. (2001) note that now, more than ever, young people desire meaningful work where they can contribute and make a difference. Like DePree, Mcgee-cooper et al. agree that building community promotes creativity, teamwork, and shared vision, ultimately leading to improved productivity and performance. Mcgee-cooper et al. pointed to the success of large corporations, such as T.D. Industries (TDI) as a model example for servant leadership. McGee-cooper et al. explained that the administration at TDI does not operate under a hierarchical system; instead, employees are viewed as valued partners and leaders. At TDI, leadership means holding the ladder for employees so they can climb to their full potential rather than having employees as direct reports.

Similarly, former CEO of Southwest Airlines, Herb Kelleher, leveraged the servant-leadership concept and enjoyed equal success. He operated from the perspective that employees come first, and the organization's success is the by-product (Mcgee-cooper et al., 2001). Adding to the findings of McGee-Cooper et al., other studies found a correlation between the behaviors of CEOs and the implications it has on middle managers and frontline workers (Khuwaja et al., 2020; Yang et al., 2021). The study concluded that the CEO's servant behavior substantially impacted the organization's and employees' performances.

Servant Leadership in Educational Institutions

In *"The Adult Learner,"* Knowles et al. (2005) suggested that the mutuality between teachers and students as joint inquirers is salient in the learning process, and with a servant teacher, both benefit from the experience with a greater appreciation and deeper insights. Knowles et al. suggested that there are six principles a learner goes through to achieve social and individual growth; the six principles are as follows: (1) Need to know: A learner needs to know why he is asked to learn, (2) Self-concept: Is the learner motivated to learn? (3) Experience of the learner: Is the learner familiar with the topic he is engaged in? (4) Readiness to learn: Does the learner have the ability and maturity to learn? (5) Orientation to learning: Will learning something new help solve a problem? (6) Motivation to learn: Is there a reward for learning? Applying the principles requires disrupting traditional teaching methods by shifting from teacher to facilitator—the servant aspect of servant leadership (Knowles et al., 2005). In this way, teachers are responsible for the students and their progress. More specifically, when teachers become facilitators, they shift from content transmitters to supervisors or resource managers, affecting the teacher and learners' mindset.

In *"Teacher as Servant Applications of Greenleaf's Servant Leadership in Higher Education,"* Hays (2008) agrees that servant-leadership or the servant-teaching model gives voice to the students and places the needs of the students as a priority. He posits that continuing to teach in ways that replicate command-and-control, hierarchy, and power to coerce compliance rather than autonomy is detrimental at a time when creativity, empowerment, and collaboration are essential. Servant Leadership has exploded into the world of higher education as a pragmatic leadership approach to teaching and developing faculties, staff, and students (Aboramadan et al., 2020; Berry, 2015; Bowman, 2005; Hays, 2008; Hutapea, 2022; Kiersch & Peters, 2017; Melinda & Antonio, 2019). The implication is that with a caring and supporting faculty, students are more likely to reach their full potential, enrich their lives, and make impactful contributions to employers, society, and the world (Kiersch & Peters, 2017).

Moreover, Hays (2008) argues that traditional teaching methods are robotic, impersonal, and a disservice to students. Furthermore, conventional learning methods inadequately prepare students for the workforce but, more importantly, fail to develop graduates' leadership skills. In a qualitative study, shifting from teacher-centered to student-centered using servant leadership principles, Hays found positive reactions from students and teachers when servant leadership was applied—using the servant-leadership principles within an education environment. Hays introduced the concept of *"servant teacher"* and identified the servant characteristics of empathy, commitment to growth, stewardship, and building community as practical applications in the classroom. Finally, Hays observed that when teachers' roles change from autocratic leaders to servant teachers, student engagement improves with a more profound appreciation for one another, and learning becomes more meaningful.

In *Teacher as Servant Leader*, Bowman (2005) directly connects Greenleaf's original observation and institutions of higher learning. That is, "Do those served grow as persons? Do they, while being served, become healthier, wiser, freer, more autonomous, and more likely themselves to become servants?" (Greenleaf, 1977, p. 13). Bowman and others (Irving, 2005; Jennings & Stahl-Wert, 2016; Wheeler, 2012) draw from the principles of Greenleaf's writing as part of a woven fabric to illustrate the connectivity between teachers, students, and the outcome of a masterpiece work of art. This arabesque artwork captures the essence of students yearning to reach their full potential, to become more as teachers become more supportive and inspiring, and together, transforming conventional teacher-student relationships in the process (Bowman, 2005; Greenleaf, 1977; Wheeler, 2012).

In his book, "*Servant Leadership for Higher Education: Principles and Practices,*" Wheeler observed that meeting the needs of students (those being served) should be the primary objective of teachers and professional staff (servant leaders). While others suggest that servant leadership may not be the panacea for some unforgiving universities—racially and culturally influenced universities—the tide has turned, and more universities are opting for a more accommodating and supportive environment for all learners, which means an increase in faculty concerns for moralities and relationships. Leaders command influence, and in education, faculties are leaders that influence student behaviors. Mclinda and Antonio (2019) studied servant leadership in higher education and found a high correlation between faculty morality and relationships in public and private universities, respectively. In their study, a large number of participants, such as Department Heads (46%), Program Directors (32%), and Dean and Vice Dean (10%), were surveyed. The participation of these individuals was significant, and the outcome had tremendous implications because, in higher education institutions, these individuals are responsible for faculty and student success. The authors encourage universities to adopt a servant leadership approach to promulgate leadership development and enhance students' learning experiences.

Erkutlu and Chafra (2015) made an exciting connection between servant leadership and voice behavior. The authors suggest that servant leadership promulgates trust, and trust involves risk-taking. In other words, when followers trust their leader, they will take more risks to please the leader. Similarly, in an educational environment, when students trust their teacher, they are more likely to be engaged in critical discussions and express their opinions—voice behavior (Erkutlu & Chafra, 2015). In a separate study, Premeaux and Bedeian (2015) examined employee self-esteem and supervisor trust and found that many employees hesitated to voice their opinions for fear of retaliation. The fear of risk-taking or interpersonal risks psychologically impacts individual behaviors and how the individual reacts.

Whereas those who trusted their supervisor were more likely to express their opinion on work-related issues without fear (van Dierendonck, 2011). While this is not a new phenomenon, it makes sense because many students who need more self-confidence or are struggling with the English language are unlikely to speak up in an open forum. However, if the students perceive their teacher as caring, supportive, fair, and trustworthy, they will likely voice their opinions without fear of ridicule. The study by Erkutlu and Chafra supports faculty servant leadership and its effect on voice behavior. Greenleaf's concern for institutions, particularly education and business, has inspired servant leaders, from teachers to CEOs. Another category in which servant leadership is consistently practiced is religious institutions. The research discusses servant leadership in religious institutions as follows.

Servant Leadership in Religious Institutions

The concept behind servant leadership is to serve first (Greenleaf, 1977). In *"Transitioning to a Servant Leadership Culture Through the Teachings of Jesus,"* Craun and Henson (2022) analyzed the relationship between servant leadership and gospel scriptures. The authors agreed that servant leadership improves organizations; moreover, the authors posited that gospel scriptures inspire and promulgate morale and improve job satisfaction because individuals feel a sense of pride in service to God. Their research revealed that servant leadership is valuable to the institution because servant leaders focus on the growth and development of others. Similarly, religious leaders have used pericopes from the bible to validate the application of servant leadership by using passages from nearly every book in the bible to tell stories of different servants, such as Abraham and Joseph in the book of Genesis or Moses in the book of Exodus, or Matthew, Peter, Paul, and others, for example, performing services for the greater good all in the name of God (Crowther, 2018).

In *Biblical Servant Leadership: An Exploration of Leadership for the Contemporary Context,* Crowther (2018) connects servant leadership with clergy in churches, citing the concept of a servant-first practice; a clergy first desires to serve and then makes a conscious choice to lead. Crowther explains that churches are needed to serve people and help them heal, and if church leaders can become servant leaders, they can set an example for other institutions, which may help society at large. In growing church organizations, pericopes from the bible, more specifically Matthew 20:28 and Matthew 28:19, are often used to set the foundation for why listening, giving a voice, and prioritizing service first are essential as believers of Christ. Service to others was emphasized in the former scripture, and disciples were encouraged to create more servants in the latter. In essence, the servants mentioned in the pericope prioritized serving God, and in following

God, they learned to lead with a servant's heart (Craun & Henson, 2022; Greenleaf, 1977). Crowther concludes that a better society begins with servant leaders committed to the growth and development of people in the organization.

The principles of servant leadership are well documented, explored, and propounded, e.g., *listening, empathy, foresight, and stewardship* (Crowther, 2015; Greenleaf, 1977; Spears, 1998). Others have attempted to shorten, modify, and redefine principles of servant leaders as altruistic, wisdom, calling, and persuasive, to name a few (Barbuto & Wheeler, 2006; Coggins & Bocarnea, 2015; Ebener & O'Connell, 2010), but the outcome did not deviate from Greenleaf's vision of a servant-leader, which is the desire to serve first and help followers reach their full potential. Craun and Henson (2022) found the service concept rather salient in bible scriptures and servant-leadership. Christian values and principles are critical in recruiting, retaining, and growing congregations. Locke (2019) suggested applying servant leadership for Christians and other faith-based organizations relies on applicable scriptural texts to validate servant leadership. Therefore, church ministers, preachers, and congregation leaders embodied the concept of servant leadership in their sermons and how they lived and led. In *The Impact of Servant Leadership to Followers' Psychological Capital: A Comparative Study of Evangelical Christian leader-follower Relationships in the United States and Cambodia,* Coggins and Bocarnea (2015) examined the relationship between servant leadership and the positive effect on followers—psychological capital—with Evangelical Christians in the United States and Cambodia. To be clear, psychological capital refers to an individual's "hope, self-efficacy, optimism, and resilience" (Coggins & Bocarnea, 2015, p. 113). Based on the study, the authors found that servant leaders positively increase followers' well-being—psychological capital. Servant leadership must accompany deep values and principles, and faith-based organizations believe these values and principles have long been inculcated in followers of Christ since Genesis. Servant leadership is critical in strengthening people and organizations, from religious institutions to government entities. Next, the study examines the influence of servant leadership in government agencies.

Servant Leadership in Governmental Agencies

Great leaders inspire actions and give hope to people in challenging and uncertain times. Leaders rise to the occasion, challenge the status quo, and overcome difficult situations; in essence, true leaders, Burns (2012) suggested, beg crisis because it is when true greatness emerges. However, are servant leaders the types of leaders to fill this void? Seminal works by James McGregor Burns (1978) postulated that transformational leaders are more suitable for organizations because of their ability to envision and inspire trust in followers. In other words, Burns suggests transformational leaders consider the values, needs, and beliefs of those being led. Bernard Bass (1985) added that transformational leaders bring awareness to followers through vision and confidence. Nevertheless, some leaders lean toward transactional leadership because they are task-oriented and procedural-driven (Kuhnert & Lewis, 1987). Still, others argued that transactional leadership provides mutual understanding because both leader and follower gain something of value—an exchange of outcomes (Yukl, 2012). So, what role do servant-leaders serve in government organizations, specifically law enforcement? The study examines the emaciated topic of servant-leadership in law enforcement and closely related professions.

In the military, transactional and autocratic leaders are the norm because the job requires leaders to command, control, direct, and accomplish missions without much input from followers, if any—this is particularly true in wartime and hostile situations or environments (Roberts, 2018). In *Twelve Principles of Modern Military Leadership*, Roberts suggests that leaders should lead from the front to set an example for followers and to command respect, the first of the twelve principles. The remaining principles are Self-confidence, Moral Courage, Physical Courage, Foster Teamwork, Fitness, and Energy, Aggressive, and Bold, Take Care of Your Soldiers, being a Student of the Past, being Decisive, Show Determination, and having Strong Character. Roberts concludes that leaders deficient in one or more of the abovementioned principles will have a "detrimental effect on mission success, morale, and the efficacy of leadership" (p. 6).

Similarly, law enforcement has mimicked the command-and-control leadership style for organizational effectiveness for the greater part of the last century (Cordner, 1978; Jermier & Berkes, 1979; Moore, 1976). The few scholastic works of literature that provide evidence of servant leadership related to paramilitary organizations are confined to qualitative study and, perhaps, are more of an afterthought than actual findings. In *Servant Leadership in the Military,* Turner and Hamstra (2018) conducted qualitative research using current and former military officers and their perspectives on servant leadership. In one of the interviews, a participant explained that he prefers participative and laissez-faire leadership style because it is less stressful; however, the same participant also stated he would be interested in learning more about servant leadership if it helps improve relationships with the troops. Turner and Hamstra suggested that servant leadership can be combined with the armed forces' values of duty, honor, and country to create more effective leaders in the military. The authors argued that with servant leadership, the armed forces would likely retain highly skilled individuals (retention), improve morale, help people achieve maximum potential, and encourage creativity and engagement.

In a different study, Earnhardt (2008) attempted to determine if servant leadership existed among military members of the Arm Forces (Air Force, Navy, Army, Marines, and Coast Guard), using a servant leadership instrument designed by Dennis and Bocarnea (2005)—a tool to measure effectiveness based on servant leadership characteristics. In this mixed methods study, Earnhardt tested the servant leadership theory against Patterson's (2003) servant leadership paradigm, which suggests that to become a servant leader, one must begin with love (agapao love—a complete person with wants, needs, and desires) and traverse through four phases—humility, altruism, vision, and trust—leading to empowerment and ultimately, service to others. Earnhardt's study concluded that there was a positive causal relationship between servant-leadership in the military and Patterson's servant-leadership model.

In a more recent study by Bahmani et al. (2021), the authors attempted to validate servant leadership in a military context by observing military leaders' antecedents, behaviors, and outcomes. They hypothesized: "What are the behavioral dimensions of servant leadership in a military context? What are the antecedents for the incidence of servant leadership behavior in a military context? What are the outcomes of using servant leadership behavior?" (Bahmani et al., 2021, pp. 66-67). Specifically, the study participants and location were Iranian veterans in southern Iran. In the study, participants pointed to three specific personalities that impacted their response to their leader. First, the Commander was knowledgeable, experienced in military operations, and had networking power. Second, the Commanders possessed political acumen; they understood why they were involved in combat and needed to defend their country. Lastly, the third personality trait that participants observed from their Commander was emotional intelligence; participants valued understanding and emotional and mental support from the leader. Interestingly, in their 2021 qualitative study, Bahmani et al. discovered that servant leaders (military leaders) expressed serving followers first rather than commanding them in times of war. Moreover, they found that leaders with high religious values treat their colleagues and subordinates better.

However, unlike the military, law enforcement leaders spend more time engaging employees and citizens in the community with fewer situations that call for war-like tactics.

Thomas and Cangemi (2021) conducted a recent study on law enforcement leadership skills and their impact on subordinates and community members. The authors examined authoritarian, transactional, and transformational leadership styles. However, the study did not include servant leadership—nonexistent in law enforcement—thus giving rise to the importance of the topic. It provided evidence of a gap in research, specifically servant leadership in law enforcement. In their study, Thomas and Cangemi (2021) observed some of the characteristics of law enforcement and described the saliency of trust and engagement for law enforcement leaders. They proposed that subordinates should be involved in the decision-making process and allowed to contribute to policy and procedural changes within the organization. Furthermore, the authors concluded that lacking trust and engagement leads to low morale and high turnover. In contrast, organizations that foster participatory decision-making, empowerment, and nurturing enjoy high success, low turnover, and a trusting environment. Thomas and Cangemi's findings reinforce Greenleaf's (1977) servant-leadership principles of listening and building community—hence, participatory decision-making and a trusting environment.

In the same study, Thomas and Cangemi (2021) asserted that authoritarian leaders fuel resistance and are negatively associated with performance outcomes. At the same time, transactional leaders are goal-oriented individuals and may subject followers to punishment when goals are not met and priorities are not aligned. Bass (1990) suggested that while transactional leadership may appear practical, it is a prescription for mediocrity. Lastly, while transformational leadership has most servant-leadership principles, it does not prioritize service to others—serving first. Thomas and Cangemi suggested that transformational leadership positively correlated with employee outcomes, job satisfaction, high commitment, and low turnover. However, the caveat to transformational leadership is tied to a substantial group culture; lacking culture, commitment may fall short (Shim et al., 2015).

Of the three leadership styles reviewed by Thomas and Cangemi (2021), transformational leadership was more effective in law enforcement for employee engagement and creating a trusting environment. Finally, the studies suggested that future research should address barriers to policing and other alternatives that improve relationships between the police and the community. This research highlighted several entities where servant leadership was implemented and positively impacted the people and organizations. However, the conceptualization of servant leadership is not without critiques; the final section of this research acknowledges and discusses several critiques of servant leadership.

Critiques of Servant Leadership

Several scholars have suggested that servant leadership has some fundamental problems. Interestingly, while servant leadership has been shown to improve trust, relationships, performances, and productivity (Chen et al., 2015; Lee et al., 2020; Miao et al., 2014b; van Dierendonck & Nuijten, 2011), others believe servant leadership and the servant's heart conceptualization is vulnerable and exploitable, particularly when leading Machiavellians— individuals with dark traits (Wisse & Sleebos, 2016). The following literature and journals share a different side of servant-leadership, suggesting servant-leaders are vulnerable and susceptible to followers with harmful intentions.

In a study in the Journal of Work and Organizational Psychology, Fatima et al. (2021) postulated that calculative and manipulative individuals could easily exploit servant leaders to achieve career advancement or gain social power. According to Fatima et al. (2021), the authors believe that because servant leaders prioritize serving first, the opportunity for manipulation by self-motivated followers is great. The authors highlighted the servant aspect of servant leadership and suggested that rather than concentrating on influence—a general definition of leadership—servant leaders accentuate the conceptualization of service. Moreover, the authors argued that the core value of servant leadership is the servant's heart, which underlies humbleness and putting the priorities of others first before self. Furthermore, Fatima et al. point to other studies that suggest humans are inherently selfish and have a manipulative inner desire (Diebels et al., 2018; Dubois et al., 2015; Force, 2003; Yu, 2011). The authors argued that followers could exploit and manipulate such servant leaders to achieve career advancement or social status because servant leaders trust their followers and tend to have amicable relationships with them. Fatima et al. further argued that servant-leader behavior provides a breeding ground for opportunistic and manipulative individuals, particularly Machiavellianism—individuals with self-interest and known to be exploitative for personal gain (Fatima et al., 2021; Harms & Spain, 2015; Jonason & Webster, 2010; Wisse & Sleebos, 2016). Fatima et al. focused on Machiavellianism traits because of the vulnerability of servant leaders and Machiavellianism's link to deceptions. The study concluded that servant leaders are linked to improving employee outcomes but are vulnerable under high-Machiavellian followers.

Next, the veil of servant leadership or the dark side of servant leadership can mask the authenticity of true servant leaders (Camm, 2019). In his article, *The Dark Side of Servant Leadership,* Camm discussed the dark, darker, and darkest side of servant leadership and the challenges of identifying the true identity of a servant leader. For instance, when leaders attain rank or leadership positions without proper qualifications, Camm argued that those leaders lack knowledge and skills, and those very same skills impede their awareness—the dark side. The author continues, suggesting that some leaders mask paternalistic leadership as servant leadership—the darker side. Camm proposed that this trap encourages followers to react in a childlike manner, which is the antithesis of servant leadership. Therefore, this means that followers of the former (paternalistic leadership) depend on the leader. In contrast, followers of the latter (servant leadership) are more autonomous and likely to become servants (leaders) themselves (Greenleaf, 1977). Furthermore, Camm observed that in some cases, skilled manipulators (authoritarian leaders) would resort to any means necessary to gain compliance by masking control-centric tactics with servant leadership vocabulary—the darkest side. Servant leadership fosters healing and community-building (Greenleaf, 1977), and according to Camm, power-seeking individuals will mask whatever is necessary as servanthood to gain power. These narcissistic individuals are cunning, arrogant, and destructive (Camm, 2019).

Servant leadership has become a household name for many organizations as the preferred method for improving employee engagement and increasing organizational productivity (Birch, 2002; Chen et al., 2015; Coggins & Bocarnea, 2015; Joseph & Winston, 2005; Liden et al., 2014). However, in *When a servant-leader comes knocking...,* Andersen (2009) contends that servant leadership has not been empirically vetted, and some researchers found servant leadership less than desirable in organizational outcomes. In the journal article, Andersen distinguishes between serving the organization and followers. He suggested that the intent of leading (and leaders) is to serve the organization; in contrast, he points out that there is a direct conflict when servant leaders' priority shifts from serving the organization to serving followers. He argued that this practice of servant leadership places the organization on the back burner as secondary rather than a primary concern.

Interestingly, Andersen (2009) professed that the leader-follower relationship does not exist in business management. Instead, the relationship is manager-employee because employees are paid to help attain organizational goals. Furthermore, Andersen suggests that followers are volunteers willing to follow without compensation. To this end, Andersen agrees that the concept of servant leadership is meant to help personnel develop and achieve their full potential. Whereas managers are responsible for organizational effectiveness, and organizational goals can only be attained by subordinates (paid employees), not followers.

In a different study, Palumbo (2016) suggested that servant leadership is a disadvantage for nonprofit organizations. While Palumbo agrees that leadership is necessary and critical for organizational success, he argues that servant leadership creates an environment for dependency, discouraging proactive behavior. Consistent with other studies (Andersen, 2009; Burns, 1978; Deluga & Souza, 1991; Kuhnert & Lewis, 1987), Palumbo's position is based on a predefined definition of leadership—one that equips, trains, and influences as defined by Winston and Patterson (2006)—which assumes a transactional relationship exists between followers and leaders. Therefore, this relationship makes organizational success transactional, meaning there is an exchange of value for the service performed. More specifically, Northouse (2012) explained the leadership process as being transactional and suggested that the transaction is where the leader and followers affect each other and is an interactive event.

From a transactional perspective, the servant leader must manage followers with technical and financial resources to enhance organizational effectiveness (Palumbo 2016, as cited in Bass & Bass, 2009). In a qualitative study of servant leadership, Palumbo pointed out that one of the respondents felt unprepared to make decisions without the leader's affirmation. Furthermore, in the same study, Palumbo claimed that servant leaders, as suggested by Greenleaf (1977)—servant first, might do more to constrain followers when they are not present rather than empowering followers. Palumbo argued that servant-leadership's side effects are that followers become reliant on the leader, and instead of becoming autonomous, they become less proactive. Rather than reaching their full potential, they are less likely to become servant leaders. The author suggests clarity in defining both theoretical and empirical servant leadership, which may help shed light on the negatives of servant leadership.

Summary

Leaders inspire, rally, and unify others for the greater good. Great leaders give people hope because they rise to the challenge and overcome difficult situations. Law enforcement organizations are facing extreme turbulence in a tumultuous climate. While the call from critics and advocacy groups to defund law enforcement is not a viable option, reimagining law enforcement leadership is overdue. However, empirical studies of law enforcement leaders and leadership styles have left much to be desired. Currently, there is limited empirical documentation of servant leadership and its impact on law enforcement organizations. Therefore, further research in this discipline is necessary and warranted. The research synthesized the work of Robert Greenleaf and others on servant leadership and its impact on business, higher education, religious groups, and government agencies. This research is necessary to provide readers with a broad understanding of servant leadership and those arguing against it.

Law and order are necessary to keep the peace in a civil society; therefore, those responsible for law enforcement must prioritize service. Servant leadership prioritizes people and helps them grow to their full potential (Greenleaf, 1977). The leader as the servant—servant leadership—was conceptualized by Robert Greenleaf during a tumultuous time in history. Greenleaf was concerned about the country's future and the young people who would someday lead this great nation. As Robert Greenleaf contemplated building a more just society, he was inspired by a short novel by Herman Hesse, "*Journey to the East*." The message extracted from

Journey to the East is that a leader must desire to serve first before leading someone. In doing so, priority is placed on service and helping people reach their full potential. Law enforcement exists to provide a service to the public. In this climate of civil unrest, chaos, and unbalanced order, the priority must be focused on serving others—service first.

The compilation of the literature centers around the topic of leadership, servant leadership. As illustrated throughout this chapter, servant-leadership paradigm has been successfully implemented in many disciplines, such as business, higher education, religion, military, and nonprofit and for-profit organizations (Allen et al., 2018; Chen et al., 2015; Coggins & Bocarnea, 2015; Crowther, 2018; Lee et al., 2020; Locke, 2019; Miao et al., 2014b; Palumbo, 2016; van Dierendonck, 2011). However, limited literature resources were found on law enforcement and servant leadership, specifically how servant leadership impacts job satisfaction in law enforcement. The lack of literature on this topic suggests that more research is needed and validates the saliency of this study. While the interest in servant-leadership has brought new excitement to leaders in various institutions, only some are convinced of the *servant-as-leader* concept. In fact, many are critical of the vulnerability of being a servant and serving those less than genuine, those with bad intentions, and those who are self-serving. Moreover, others suggest it is lip service because servant leadership is neither theoretical nor practical (Bradley, 1999; Camm, 2009). Still, others contend that servant leadership is undefined and lacks empirical support (Andersen, 2009; Stone, Russell, & Patterson, 2004). The concept of servant leadership is difficult for some to accept; nonetheless, the principle and practice of servant leadership is one interpretation of leadership, and it is not meant to be all-encompassing. Northouse (2012) reminds readers that the definition of leadership is elusive, and there is no one best definition.

At the heart of every leader lies the desire to serve. Similarly, in the heart of every law enforcement individual lies a strong desire to protect and serve. Servant leadership is a good leadership style that promulgates trust, service, and community. Moreover, servant leadership is viable as law enforcement leaders face increasingly hostile and conflict-laden environments, low morale, high turnover, and mistrust. The literature review has three objectives: First, to provide context to servant leadership; second, to examine existing literature for and against the conceptualization of servant leadership; and third, to examine how servant leadership affects employee perceptions and leader trust and how employee perceptions impact performances and job satisfaction in law enforcement. Chapter Three will discuss the research procedures and methodology, research paradigm, research design, sampling procedures and data collection, and statistical tests.

PART FOUR:
The Procedures and Methodology

The previous section reviewed servant leadership as conceptualized by Robert Greenleaf and how he envisioned servant leaders—leaders who are servants. In Part Three, we continued with the review of the seminal work by Greenleaf, namely his essays on servant leadership. Servant leadership is not an emergent paradigm; in fact, many industries—TDI, Southwest Airline, and Herman Miller Furniture Company—have been influenced by and succeeded with the concept of servant leadership (DePree, 2002; Ladkin & Taylor, 2010; Spears, 1998). The praxes of servant leadership have inspired leaders from various industries, including businesses, higher education institutions, government agencies, and religious organizations. Part Three summarizes the concept of servant leadership in each industry mentioned above and how the servant leadership concept transformed the organizations. According to Greenleaf (1977), servant leadership shifts the focus from organizational success to individual achievements, helping elevate individuals beyond what they initially thought was possible. The ten characteristics of servant leadership were identified and explained based on Greenleaf's (1977) original work and interpretations by Spears (1998) to set the foundation and expand general knowledge on the constructs of servant leadership.

The research acknowledges the strengths and weaknesses of servant leadership; accordingly, a section of Part Three was dedicated to critiques of servant leadership. The literature review includes published literature, peer-reviewed journals, and quantitative studies. While many see servant leadership as a viable option for increasing employee engagement, strengthening relationships, and fostering a growth environment, others vehemently disagree (Andersen, 2009; Camm, 2019; Palumbo, 2016; Stone, Russell, & Patterson, 2003). In this section, other scholars challenged the effectiveness of servant leadership and whether the concept of a servant leader is appropriate in leading businesses, educational institutions, government agencies, and religious organizations (Fatima et al., 2021; Harms & Spain, 2015; Jonason & Webster, 2010;

Wisse & Sleebos, 2016). The literature review concludes with contrasting perspectives and acknowledging critiques of servant leadership.

The review acknowledges servant leadership's impact on industries and respects the opposing perspectives. However, limited literature exists examining the correlation between servant leadership and its impact on law enforcement. Servant leadership has the potential to cultivate, inspire, and foster an inclusive and equitable work environment that is conducive to growth (Blanchard, 2019; Maxwell, 2007). To this end, the limited literature on servant leadership in law enforcement suggests a need and necessity to address the gap. In Part Four, we illustrate the research design to address the literature gap that references servant leadership and its impact on the law enforcement industry. Therefore, Part Four includes the research paradigm, research design, sampling procedures, and the implementation of statistical tests.

Research Paradigm

This research employs a quantitative approach design. Servant leadership has been studied and successfully implemented in various industries—higher education, private and public businesses, religious institutions, and government organizations (Allen et al., 2018; Berry, 2015; Charles, 2015; Bowman, 2005; Kiersch & Peters, 2017; Mcgee-cooper et al., 2001; Turner & Hamstra, 2018). In a qualitative study, Bahmani et al. (2021) found that military leaders expressed the need to serve followers rather than traditional command-and-control leadership. Additionally, from a Christianity perspective, Coggins and Bocarnea (2015) found that servant leaders enhanced followers' well-being. The literature analysis in Part Three included several studies from each industry, as mentioned earlier, promulgating servant leadership.

However, while Parts Two and Three attempted to uncover the impact of servant leadership in multiple industries, studies on the correlation between servant leadership and its impact on law enforcement was limited. The literature review also uncovered that most servant leadership studies were qualitative designs, except for a few. Furthermore, very few specific studies targeted the correlation between servant leadership and law enforcement. There are deficiencies in past literature on servant leadership and law enforcement. The law enforcement population has largely been ignored in published literature connecting servant leadership and law enforcement leaders. This research uses a quantitative design approach to examine the relationship between servant leadership and law enforcement organizations. According to Creswell and Creswell (2018), quantitative research "is an approach for testing objective theories by examining the relationship among variables" (p. 4). In this case, the variables are officers, deputies, and front-line supervisors. This quantitative study design approach hopes to add to and advance servant leadership in a profession that has largely been neglected in the research community—law enforcement.

Research Design

Based on the four research questions, this research design falls under the nonexperimental correlation and causal-comparative category, which does not call for manipulating one or more variables. This quantitative study follows a postpositivist worldview in that it reflects the need to identify and assess the perceptions and attitudes of a sample population (Creswell & Creswell, 2018; Phillips & Burbules, 2000). More specifically, a quantitative design allows the data collection—through a measurement instrument—to be analyzed through a statistical process and hypotheses under investigation (Creswell & Creswell, 2018). Additionally, the nonexperimental correlation "provides a quantitative description of trends, attitudes, and opinions of a population…by studying a sample of that population," (Creswell & Creswell, 2018, p. 147), and causal-comparative examines variables with two or more groups or levels for one or more dependent variables. To be clear, this quantitative study—a survey design—aims to evaluate whether servant leadership characteristics were perceived by a subgroup through a self-administered process. The survey research design is the most efficient method of gathering data from multiple law enforcement agencies with a large sample population (Berger, 1996; Brown & Hale, 2014; Girden & Kabacoff, 2010).

The target population for this study is law enforcement officers or deputies within the United States, and the sample was drawn from voluntary law enforcement agencies and their personnel, excluding management-level employees. The exclusion of management was intentional because the study aimed to examine perceptions of servant leadership characteristics from the perspectives of officers, deputies, and front-line supervisors. This quantitative—non-experimental correlation and causal-comparative—study explores the relationships of two or more variables through correlational analysis. First, the quantitative study research question examined to what extent do characteristics of the six subscales of servant leadership behavior (*values people, develops people, builds community, displays authenticity, provides leadership, shares leadership*) correlate with the perceptions of police officers, deputy sheriffs, and frontline supervisors regarding job satisfaction. Second, the research question examined whether there is a correlation between servant leadership and job satisfaction based on the agency size. For the second question, two agencies were selected based on their agency size: (a) 50 or more officers but less than 500 and (b) 500 or more officers. Third, the research question examined job satisfaction and what differences exist based on years of service; the fourth question examined what differences exist in job satisfaction based on the participants' levels of education.

The first two research questions required a minimum sample size of 60 per the University of the Cumberlands' Quantitative Design for Dissertation Research guidelines (Graduate School Doctoral Handbook, 2022). The non-experimental correlation design explores the relationships between two or more variables through correlational analysis. To determine the sample size needed for the third and fourth research questions, G*Power software (version 3.1.9.7; Faul, Erdfelder, Lang, & Buchner, 2007) was used to calculate the minimum sample size. This calculation assumed an alpha coefficient of .05, a medium effect size of .25, and a power of .80. According to the sample size calculation generated by G*Power, and given that there were two groups, a minimum of 128 participants were needed to address the research questions. The researcher aimed to surpass the minimum requirement and submitted 1,254 surveys to two law enforcement agencies, generating 287 responses. The researcher excluded management-level responses, which accounted for nine surveys, leaving 278 valid responses.

Organizational Leadership Assessment

The descriptive survey used for this research was the Organizational Leadership Assessment (OLA) instrument developed by Dr. James Laub (1999). According to Laub (1999), the OLA instrument survey is versatile and applicable to individuals, groups, or an entire organization. Permission was sought and granted for the use of OLA (see Appendix G). The OLA instrument solicits responses from the sample population with predefined categories, allowing the researcher to interpret inferable data results. The OLA uses six sub-scores relevant to the pre-identified areas of servant leadership characteristics (*Values People, Develops People, Builds Community, Displays Authenticity, Provides Leadership, Shares Leadership*). The six sub-scores or constructs are defined as follows (Laub, 1999):

1. Values People: listening, serving, and trusting in people.

2. Develops People: provide opportunities, model the way, and lift others.

3. Builds Community: collaborating, building relationships, and valuing differences.

4. Displays Authenticity: holds people accountable, trustworthy, and open to new ideas.

5. Provides Leadership: one who takes initiative, is forward-thinking, and clarifies goals.

6. Shares Leadership: shared vision, democratic decision-making process, equal representation at all levels.

The OLA survey instrument was selected because it meets the objectives of this research, which is to examine whether servant leadership characteristics of the rank-and-file influence subordinates' perceptions and attitudes on job satisfaction and whether servant leadership is more prevalent in small or large agencies (law enforcement) and do perceptions vary based on years of service and education levels.

The independent variable considered for the quantitative study was sworn law enforcement personnel at the rank of police officers, deputies, and line-level supervisors. When the surveys were conducted, all officers, deputies, and line-level supervisors were considered current full-time employees of the respective law enforcement agencies. The study considered and included two law enforcement agencies meeting the criterion. The independent variable in the study defined the groups compared based on the dependent variables, perceptions of servant leadership, and job satisfaction. The dependent variables under investigation were job satisfaction based on characteristics of servant leadership and perceptions or attitudes of officers and line-level supervisors. This nonexperimental correlational and causal-comparative study seeks to examine and understand the relationship between servant leadership behaviors and job satisfaction and whether perceptions differ with tenure and education. More importantly, the study seeks to extend knowledge in an increasingly demanding profession and elucidate a topic that has been neglected in the research community.

Sampling Procedures and Data Collection Sources

Prior to initiating data collection, approval from the Institutional Review Board (IRB, see appendix D) was sought from the University of the Cumberlands in Williamsburg, Kentucky. Once IRB permission was granted, the researcher initiated the process of securing permissions from each of the selected law enforcement agencies by emailing the head of each organization or their designee to engage in the servant leadership assessment. Site authorization request forms (appendices E & F) were emailed to the department heads or designees to be signed and returned, granting permission to survey the population. Once the researcher received the completed site authorization, data collection was initiated. Data collection emanated from two law enforcement organizations; the agencies' names were provided to OLA Group, and surveys were developed specifically for those agencies. The OLA Group was responsible for the survey organization and instructional email for completing and submitting the surveys.

The OLA Group prepared the surveys and added two custom questions: (1) Please indicate your level of education—High school Graduate, Some College, Bachelor's Degree, Graduate Degree, and (2) How long have you been employed with the current agency?—1-5 years, 6-10 years, 11-15 years, 16 or more years. The custom questions were designed to answer research questions (3) What differences exist in officers' perceptions of job satisfaction based on years of service? and (4) What differences exist in officers' perceptions of job satisfaction based on the levels of education? A survey link was made available for all participants through email via a weblink connected to www.olagroup.com as required by the developer. An informed consent form (see Appendix C) was required to be viewed by all participants. All agencies were provided instructions on completing and submitting the survey by OLA Group. Participants in the survey were voluntary and granted the autonomy to complete the OLA in one sitting. In general, the OLA survey instrument took less than fifteen minutes to complete and return to the OLA Group. The Principal Researcher could monitor the assessment's progress and inform OLA Group when sufficient surveys were completed. Once the Principal Researcher determined that sufficient OLA surveys were completed by the participants, the OLA Group was notified to compile the data, and the raw data was then provided to the Principal Researcher. The data was provided in a Microsoft Excel (version 2019) spreadsheet form. The data in the Excel spreadsheet was then sorted and imported into JASP (Version 0.17; JASP Team, 2023) statistics software for analysis.

The research sought to survey law enforcement agencies with a minimum of 50 sworn personnel but no maximum number of employees. The agencies were initially separated into three categories, small, medium, and large, based on the agency size: (1) 50-250 sworn, (2) 251-500 sworn, and (3) 501 or more sworn. However, finding three agencies in the above categories proved challenging, especially those that would volunteer for the research study. Therefore, the categories of law enforcement agencies were modified to consider large agencies (500 or more officers) and small agencies (50 or more officers but less than 500). The law enforcement agencies considered for the study were either Municipal Police Departments or rural County Sheriff's Departments located within the United States; for the purpose of the study and to protect the identity of the Police or Sheriff's Departments, the agencies were identified as agency 1 and agency 2. Agency 1 has a minimum of 50 sworn officers or deputies, and Agency 2 employs 500 or more officers or deputies. The sample population was either first-line supervisors or officers and deputies. This population was selected because the intent was to examine the existence of servant leadership characteristics among the rank-and-files (individuals from the rank of lieutenant and above) and whether servant leadership characteristics influenced job satisfaction.

The data collection began with an introductory email to all potential participants, Police Chiefs, Sheriffs, and their respective professional associations, explaining the purpose of the research and the desire for volunteer participation. The email concluded by asking for the agency's voluntary participation in the study. Once the agencies agreed to engage in the study, a site authorization letter was emailed to the Agency contact person to complete and return. The agency agreement or site permission letter was required to comply with the Institutional Review Board. The OLA Group was selected to prepare the survey using the Organizational Assessment Leadership survey (Laub, 1999). The OLA Group worked directly with the Principal Researcher to ensure the survey's integrity and refined custom questions that were suitable for both parties. A survey link was emailed to the Principal Researcher and then to the agency's contact person at various times, depending on when permission to survey the agency was received. The first agency—agency 1—employed approximately 76 sworn personnel, including management staff. The second agency—agency 2—employed approximately 1,148 sworn personnel, which includes the ranks of Lieutenants, Captains, Chiefs, Assistant Sheriffs, and Sheriffs. The data was collected using Laub's (1999) OLA survey instrument. The Principal Researcher was able to monitor the progress of the assessment and relay to the OLA Group when the minimum number of participants was satisfied. Once all agencies completed the assessment and the final count was reported to OLA Group, the raw data was extracted into a Microsoft Excel (version 2019) spreadsheet and provided to the Principal Researcher for further analysis.

Demographic Variables

Law enforcement, in general, is predominantly a white male-dominated profession, and historically, the profession does not require a college degree. However, changes are occurring, and many agencies across the country are seeing more diversity in race, gender, and education

(Sklansky, 2005). To this end, various perspectives on servant leadership are salient for the study. The demographic variables considered for this study were (a) years of service and (b) education levels. Gender and race were not considered due to the underrepresentation of minorities and females in law enforcement. The study examined the varying perceptions of servant leadership and job satisfaction based on the officers' tenure and their levels of education.

Validity and Reliability

The OLA instrument was designed to assess organizational wellness and leadership (Laub, 1999). The OLA was extensively field tested and validated, and according to Laub (1999), the assessment of organizations and leadership and the six subscale scores reveal high reliability. To be sure, the OLA was distributed and field tested in 45 different organizations with over 800 participants with a reliability Cronbach-Alpha coefficient of .98 (Laub, 1999). The aforementioned reliability was based on the original design of the instrument with 74 questions. However, the instrument items were reduced from 74 to 60 to reduce the time required to complete the survey and make it more appealing to organizations considering its use (Laub, 1999). According to Laub (1999), "The reduced 60-item instrument maintains the same reliability and adherence to the foundational constructs as the longer instrument" (p. 79). Laub (1999) also conducted a validity test via a Delphi survey with renowned subject matter experts by extracting responses to questions on the construct of servant leadership characteristics.

According to Akins, Tolson, and Cole (2005), the Delphi survey is a widely accepted method for forecasting group judgments and has been validated without a theoretical model. Additionally, Laub (1999) then conducted a perceived accuracy test (Face Validity Test) of the six subscales of OLA with 100 graduate students and found strong validity. Furthermore, Laub (1999) asserts that the six subscales were appropriate for diagnosing individual leadership. Accordingly,

Creswell and Creswell (2018) add that the validity of a survey should determine whether the scores are helpful and have positive consequences in real-world practices. The OLA instrument has met the score's reliability and consistency test.

Statistical Tests

The agencies that volunteered to participate in the research provided statistical data for the study. The OLA Group collected the data using OLA survey instrumentation (Laub, 1999). The OLA Group performed the initial data collection and screening. The raw data were then provided to the Principal Researcher in a Microsoft Excel (version 2019) spreadsheet for further analysis. Basic assumptions were assessed for employee job satisfaction based on the six subscales (*Values People, Develops People, Builds Community, Displays Authenticity, Provides Leadership, Shares Leadership*). A Pearson product-moment correlation was conducted to examine job satisfaction and servant leadership for the first two questions, with an alpha coefficient of .05 as an acceptable difference. The .05 coefficient is the significance level, also referred to as the breaking point on the continuum, a widely accepted solution to a problem in social science research (Spatz, 2019). The .05 value means that the results occurred "fewer than 5 times in 100 when the null hypothesis is true" (Spatz, 2019, p. 191).

The third and fourth questions sought the differences in perspectives based on demographics. The respondents' years of service and education levels were used to predict job satisfaction based on how they responded to items 56, 58, 60, 62, 64, and 66. The variables are independent or have no relationship between demographics and employee job satisfaction in law enforcement. For this purpose, a one-way ANOVA was conducted to examine the differences between job satisfaction, service years, and education levels. The assumption is that officers with tenure or formal education may be more satisfied with their job and embrace servant leadership, whereas junior officers with less education may be less satisfied with their job and servant leadership characteristics.

The first research question asks if any correlation exists between the perceptions of servant leadership behaviors and employee job satisfaction in law enforcement.

RQ1: To what extent do characteristics of the six subscales of servant leadership behavior (values people, develops people, builds community, displays authenticity, provides leadership, shares leadership) correlate with the perceptions of police officers or deputy sheriffs regarding job satisfaction?

H_01 – There is no correlation between the servant leadership construct of valuing people and employee job satisfaction.

H_{1a} – There is a relationship between job satisfaction and the servant leadership construct of valuing people.

H_02 – There is no correlation between the servant leadership construct of developing people and employee job satisfaction.

H_{1b} – There is a relationship between job satisfaction and the servant leadership construct of developing people.

H_03 – There is no correlation between the servant leadership construct of building community and employee job satisfaction.

H_{1c} – There is a relationship between job satisfaction and the servant leadership construct of building community.

H_04 – There is no correlation between the servant leadership construct of displaying authenticity and employee job satisfaction.

H_{1d} – There is a relationship between job satisfaction and the servant leadership construct of displaying authenticity.

H_05 – There is no correlation between the servant leadership construct of providing leadership and employee job satisfaction.

H_{1e} – There is a relationship between job satisfaction and the servant leadership construct of providing leadership.

H_06 – There is no correlation between the servant leadership construct of sharing leadership and employee job satisfaction.

H_{1f} – There is a relationship between job satisfaction and the servant leadership construct of sharing leadership.

The mean level of servant leadership perceptions from all participants from the OLA survey was identified and collected to answer the first research question. The overall perceived level of servant leadership behavior scores from the OLA survey served as predictor variables for the first question. The responses to each question were rated based on a Likert scale ranging from strongly disagree (1) to strongly agreed (5). The ratings were used to examine the correlation between the six subscales of servant leadership and employee job satisfaction.

To further examine whether servant leadership impacts law enforcement agencies differently, the following research question and hypothesis explored the relationships between servant leadership and employee job satisfaction in two different agencies varying in size. The proposed question was as follows:

RQ2: Is there a correlation between servant leadership and employee job satisfaction based on the agency size: (a) 50 or more officers or deputies but less than 500 and (b) 500 or more officers or deputies?

$H_0$1 – There is no correlation between servant leadership and job satisfaction in a small agency.

H_{2a} – There is a correlation between servant leadership and job satisfaction in a small agency.

$H_0$2 – There is no correlation between servant leadership and job satisfaction in a large agency.

H_{2b} – There is a correlation between servant leadership and job satisfaction in a large agency.

The third and fourth research questions examined the differences in perceptions of servant leadership behaviors based on tenure and education levels. An assumption was made that the length of time served in an organization and formal education may influence how participants respond to the six subscales of servant leadership. The years of service and education levels were each categorized into four groups. First, years of service were grouped as follows: group 1 (1-5 years), group 2 (6-10 years), group 3 (11-15 years, and group 4 (16+ years). Second, education levels were grouped as follows: group 1 (High School), group 2 (some College), group 3 (BA/BS degree), and group 4 (MA/MS degree). The questions were as follows:

RQ3: What differences exist in officers' perceptions of servant leadership behavior based on years of service?

$H_0$1– There is no difference in officers' perceptions of job satisfaction regardless of years of service.

H_{3a} – There is a difference in how officers perceive job satisfaction based on years of service.

RQ4: What differences exist in how officers perceive job satisfaction based on their level of education?

$H_0$1- There is no difference in officers' perceptions of job satisfaction regardless of the levels of education.

H_{4a} – There is a difference in how officers perceive job satisfaction based on the levels of education.

The raw data, which included the 60 total OLA items and the six constructs scores, were provided by OLAGroup. The data were imported to JASP (version 0.17) statistical software for analysis (JASP Team, 2023). The six constructs are the subscales of servant leadership mentioned above; the total OLA score is used to determine the organization's health. The OLA report used the Likert scale of 1-5 score format to help clarify the organizational health level and whether the subscales were correlated. Part Five will present a summary of the results and descriptive data. The chapter also explains the data analysis procedures, research questions, hypotheses, and findings.

Summary

Chapter Three discussed the servant leadership framework and its prevalence and impact on organizational leadership. The Chapter also acknowledged the strengths and weaknesses of servant leadership and where research can close the gap. One neglected profession is law enforcement; to be clear, doctoral dissertations on servant leadership and law enforcement exist in limited quantities. However, scholarly journals on servant leadership and law enforcement were more elusive, and the topic remains unexplored. Chapter Three is dedicated to illustrating the research procedure, methodology of data collection, and the instrumentation used to perform the correlation and causal-comparative research. Moreover, Chapter Three detailed the following for this study: research paradigm, research design, sampling procedures and data collection processes, and the statistical tests used to analyze the data. A detailed description of the data collection process and the measurement instrument was presented in Chapter Three. The next chapter discusses the research findings, participants and research setting, and research questions and hypotheses based on inferences from statistical analysis.

PART FIVE:
The Research Findings

This quantitative study examined the attitudes and perceptions of law enforcement officers, deputies, and front-line supervisors to determine whether servant leadership behaviors and job satisfaction are significantly related. The research further examined whether demographic variables such as the size of the agency, years of service, and levels of education affect the attitudes of the law enforcement workforce. Prior servant leadership studies found positive improvements in performance and employee job satisfaction. For instance, Washington et al. (2006) found that in higher education, servant leaders affect followers' performance, which ultimately affects the organization's outcome. In another research, a community hospital found that employee satisfaction was strongly correlated with servant leadership (McCann et al., 2014). The research questions were formed during the literature review and fully developed after discovering that servant leadership in law enforcement is an under-studied topic. The research questions that guided the study are as follows:

1. To what extent do characteristics of the six subscales of servant leadership behavior (*values people, develops people, builds community, displays authenticity, provides leadership, shares leadership*) correlate with the perceptions of police officers or deputy sheriffs regarding job satisfaction?

2. Is there a correlation between servant leadership and employee job satisfaction based on the agency size: (a) 50 or more officers or deputies but less than 500 and (b) 500 or more officers or deputies?

3. Is there a difference in how officers perceive job satisfaction based on their years of service?

4. Is there a difference in how officers perceive job satisfaction based on their levels of education?

This chapter discusses the analysis of the data collected from the OLA instrument and how it ties back to the research questions. The chapter is divided into the following sections: Participants and Research Setting, Analysis of Research Questions, and Summary.

Participants and Research Setting

Research questions one and two required a minimum sample size greater than 60 with a medium effect size and an alpha coefficient of .05. To determine the sample size needed for the third and fourth research questions, G*Power software (version 3.1.9.7; Faul, Erdfelder, Lang, & Buchner, 2007) was used to calculate the minimum sample size. This calculation assumed an alpha coefficient of .05, a medium effect size of .25, and a power of .80. According to the sample size calculation generated by G*Power, and given that there were two groups, a minimum of 128 participants were needed to address the research questions. Open invitations were emailed to several law enforcement agencies throughout the United States, seeking agencies with 50 or more sworn personnel to participate in the study.

Three agencies, varying in size, were invited to participate in this research. However, one of the agencies dropped out of the study prior to initiating the survey. In total, two agencies committed to the survey with a total of 1,260 potential participants. The first agency employed 76 sworn personnel, including management, and the second had 1,184 sworn personnel, including management. The agencies were from the Midwest (agency 1) and Southwest (agency 2). In total 1, 254 surveys were emailed to the participating agencies, with 70 surveys going to Agency 1 and 1,184 surveys to Agency 2. All participants are sworn law enforcement officers. From Agency 1, the respondents returned 56 surveys, an 80% response rate, and Agency 2 had 231 surveys returned, a 20% response rate. All surveys were completed voluntarily and at each individual's place of employment during regular work hours. The total number of surveys returned combined was 287, and for this study, management was excluded, which brought the adjusted number of valid surveys to 278 ($N = 278$).

Analyses of Research Questions

The research questions were formed during the review of the literature and fully developed from the survey. Several servant leadership measurement instruments were considered, but the Organizational Leadership Assessment (OLA) was selected as the best instrument to measure servant leadership in law enforcement. The questions were designed to measure attitudes and perceptions of the workforce (officers) and frontline supervisors regarding management and whether their perceptions influenced job satisfaction. The OLA model suggests that servant leadership can be measured by how individuals respond to the six constructs, which are the subscales of servant leadership—values people, develops people, builds community, displays authenticity, provides leadership, and shares leadership (Laub, 2000). Servant leaders place the priority on serving first (Greenleaf, 1977)—putting the interests of followers before self; thus, high scores of the six subscales would indicate a high correlation with servant leadership. For the first and second questions, a Pearson product-moment correlation was conducted to examine the relationships between the six subscales of servant leadership, job satisfaction, and agency size. Questions three and four required a one-way ANOVA to examine the differences in perceptions of job satisfaction based on the demographics of tenure and levels of education.

Before analyzing the research questions, data screening and hygiene were initiated to ensure the variables of interest met the statistical assumptions. Furthermore, the variables were evaluated for missing data, outliers, and normality. JASP (Version 0.17) descriptive statistical analysis was applied to determine if there were missing data, and the frequency count indicated no missing data. Also, normality was checked in JASP statistical software with a Q-Q Plot, and no deviations were noted. Finally, the test assumptions were checked, and because of the large sample size (N = 278), the alpha level for Levene's test was set at $p < .001$. The Levene's equality of variance test was non-significant (p = .004), indicating that the assumption of homogeneity of variance was not violated.

Research Question One

RQ1: To what extent do characteristics of the six subscales of servant leadership behavior (*values people, develops people, builds community, displays authenticity, provides leadership, shares leadership*) correlate with the perceptions of police officers or deputy sheriffs regarding job satisfaction?

$H_0 1$ – There is no correlation between the servant leadership construct of valuing people and employee job satisfaction.

H_{1a} – There is a relationship between job satisfaction and the servant leadership construct of valuing people.

$H_0 2$ – There is no correlation between the servant leadership construct of developing people and employee job satisfaction.

H_{1b} – There is a relationship between job satisfaction and the servant leadership construct of developing people.

$H_0 3$ – There is no correlation between the servant leadership construct of building community and employee job satisfaction.

H_{1c} – There is a relationship between job satisfaction and the servant leadership construct of building community.

$H_0 4$ – There is no correlation between the servant leadership construct of displaying authenticity and employee job satisfaction.

H_{1d} – There is a relationship between job satisfaction and the servant leadership construct of displaying authenticity.

$H_{0}5$ – There is no correlation between the servant leadership construct of providing leadership and employee job satisfaction.

H_{1e} – There is a relationship between job satisfaction and the servant leadership construct of providing leadership.

$H_{0}6$ – There is no correlation between the servant leadership construct of sharing leadership and employee job satisfaction.

H_{1f} – There is a relationship between job satisfaction and the servant leadership construct of sharing leadership.

A Pearson product-moment was conducted to examine the relationships between job satisfaction and the characteristics of the six subscales of servant leadership (*values people, develops people, builds community, displays authenticity, provides leadership, shares leadership*). Laub's (1999) OLA instrument identified specific data sets from the 60-item questionnaire as characteristics of servant leadership. The data collected from the OLA instrument were analyzed using JASP statistical software to examine the relationships between servant leadership characteristics and job satisfaction. Based on the six constructs, the set of hypotheses sought a correlation between servant leadership and job satisfaction. The six data sets within OLA were used to answer research question 1. The subscores from items 1, 4, 9, 15, 19, 52, 54, 55, 57, and 63 were used to analyze alternative hypothesis (a). The alternative hypothesis sought a correlation between job satisfaction and servant leadership regarding valuing people. That is whether the leader respects, trusts, and listens to his subordinates, with the key tenets being believing in people, putting them first, and listening to them (Laub, 1999).

The subscores from items 20, 31, 37, 40, 42, 44, 46, 50, and 59 were used to analyze alternative hypothesis (b). The alternative hypothesis sought a correlation between job satisfaction and servant leadership with the construct of developing people. The construct of "develops people" suggests that a leader provides opportunities, coaches and mentors, and creates a learning environment for followers with the key tenets of providing growth opportunities and modeling the way (Laub, 1999).

Alternative hypothesis (c) used subscores from items 7, 8, 12, 13, 16, 18, 21, 25, 38, and 47. The alternative hypothesis sought a correlation between job satisfaction and servant leadership based on the construct of building community. Laub (1999) defined "building community" as lifting others, facilitating a team environment, and collaborating, with key tenets being relationships, teamwork, and valuing differences.

Items 3, 6, 10, 11, 23, 28, 32, 33, 35, 43, 51, and 61 were used to analyze alternative hypothesis (d). The alternative hypothesis sought a correlation between job satisfaction and servant leadership based on the construct of displaying authenticity. Displaying authenticity means admitting limitations, accepting criticism, being trustworthy, honest, and ethical, with fundamental tenets being transparent, self-aware, and integrity (Laub, 1999).

The subscores from items 2, 5, 14, 22, 27, 30, 36, 45, and 49 were used to analyze alternative hypothesis (e). The alternative hypothesis sought a correlation between job satisfaction and servant leadership based on the construct of providing leadership. To what extent do leaders provide leadership based on their vision, willingness to take risks, having clear goals and expectations, empowering others, and leading from the heart rather than positional authority—key tenets being vision, taking initiative, and clarifying goals (Laub, 1999).

The final items 17, 24, 26, 29, 34, 39, 41, 48, 53, and 65 served as the sixth construct for the alternative hypothesis (f). The alternative hypothesis sought a correlation between job satisfaction and servant leadership based on the construct of sharing leadership. Laub (199) suggested that leaders who "share leadership" empower others, use persuasion, not coercion, and do not seek self-recognition but rather share status and honor.

These findings indicated that job satisfaction strongly correlated with the six constructs of servant leadership but was more strongly related to the construct of *valuing people*, r (276) = .66, $p < .001$, than the remaining five subscales of servant leadership. A complete list of correlations is presented in Table 1.

Table 1

Correlation Matrix for Servant Leadership and Job Satisfaction ($N = 278$)

Variable		JS	VP	DP	BC	DA	PL	SL
1. JS	Pearson's r							
	p-value							
2. VP	Pearson's r	0.662 ***						
	p-value	< .001						
3. DP	Pearson's r	0.595 ***	0.910 ***					
	p-value	< .001	< .001					
4. BC	Pearson's r	0.551 ***	0.921 ***	0.899 ***				
	p-value	< .001	< .001	< .001				
5. DA	Pearson's r	0.577 ***	0.932 ***	0.939 ***	0.915 ***			
	p-value	< .001	< .001	< .001	< .001			
6. PL	Pearson's r	0.560 ***	0.853 ***	0.901 ***	0.871 ***	0.904 ***		
	p-value	< .001	< .001	< .001	< .001	< .001		
7. SL	Pearson's r	0.628 ***	0.895 ***	0.935 ***	0.874 ***	0.933 ***	0.895 ***	
	p-value	< .001	< .001	< .001	< .001	< .001	< .001	

Note. ***Correlation is statistically significant at $p < .001$.
Job Satisfaction (JS), Value People (VP), Develop People (DP), Build Community (BC), Display Authenticity (DA), Provide Leadership (PL), and Share Leadership (SL).

Research Question Two

RQ2: Is there a correlation between servant leadership and employee job satisfaction based on the agency size: (a) 50 or more officers or deputies but less than 500 and (b) 500 or more officers or deputies?

$H_0 1$ – There is no correlation between servant leadership and job satisfaction in a small agency.

H_{2a} – There is a correlation between servant leadership and job satisfaction in a small agency.

$H_0 2$ – There is no correlation between servant leadership and job satisfaction in a large agency.

H_{2b} – There is a correlation between servant leadership and job satisfaction in a large agency.

Agency 1 was identified as a small agency having at least 50 sworn officers but less than 500. A total of 70 surveys were sent to the agency, and 56 surveys were returned (an 80% response). One survey was considered a management-level response and, therefore, excluded. Agency1 has a valid sample size of 55 ($N = 55$). A Pearson product-moment correlation was performed for Agency 1 to examine if there was a correlation between the characteristics of servant leadership and job satisfaction. In Agency 1, overall, there were statistically significant relationships between job satisfaction and the six constructs of servant leadership, but job satisfaction was more strongly related to the construct of *building community*, $r\,(53) = .67$, $p < .001$, than the other five constructs. A complete list of correlations for Agency 1 is presented in Table 2.

Table 2

Correlation Matrix for Servant Leadership and Job Satisfaction Agency 1 ($N = 55$)

Variable		JS	VP	DP	BC	DA	PL	SL
1. JS	Pearson's r							
	p-value							
2. VP	Pearson's r	0.634 ***						
	p-value	< .001						
3. DP	Pearson's r	0.608 ***	0.938 ***					
	p-value	< .001	< .001					
4. BC	Pearson's r	0.672 ***	0.951 ***	0.929 ***				
	p-value	< .001	< .001	< .001				
5. DA	Pearson's r	0.596 ***	0.957 ***	0.963 ***	0.931 ***			
	p-value	< .001	< .001	< .001	< .001			
6. PL	Pearson's r	0.611 ***	0.864 ***	0.875 ***	0.871 ***	0.902 ***		
	p-value	< .001	< .001	< .001	< .001	< .001		
7. SL	Pearson's r	0.660 ***	0.918 ***	0.943 ***	0.929 ***	0.943 ***	0.911 ***	
	p-value	< .001	< .001	< .001	< .001	< .001	< .001	

Note. ***Correlation is statistically significant at $p < .001$.

Agency 2 was identified as a large agency having 500 or more sworn personnel. A total of 1,184 surveys were sent to the agency, and 231 surveys were returned (a 20% response). Eight surveys were considered management-level responses, which were excluded, leaving Agency 2 with a sample size of 223 valid responses ($N = 223$). A Pearson product-moment correlation was performed for Agency 2 to examine if there was a correlation between the six constructs of servant leadership and job satisfaction. Similar to Agency 1, overall, there were statistically significant relationships between the six constructs of servant leadership and job satisfaction. However, job satisfaction was more strongly related to the construct of *valuing people*, r (221) = .63, $p < .001$, than the remaining five constructs. A complete list of correlations for Agency 2 is presented in Table 3.

Table 3

Correlation Matrix for Servant Leadership and Job Satisfaction Agency 2 ($N = 223$)

Variable		JS	VP	DP	BC	DA	PL	SL
1. JS	Pearson's r							
	p-value							
2. VP	Pearson's r	0.638 ***						
	p-value	< .001						
3. DP	Pearson's r	0.559 ***	0.881 ***					
	p-value	< .001	< .001					
4. BC	Pearson's r	0.488 ***	0.895 ***	0.861 ***				
	p-value	< .001	< .001	< .001				
5. DA	Pearson's r	0.538 ***	0.911 ***	0.913 ***	0.884 ***			
	p-value	< .001	< .001	< .001	< .001			
6. PL	Pearson's r	0.511 ***	0.814 ***	0.878 ***	0.833 ***	0.876 ***		
	p-value	< .001	< .001	< .001	< .001	< .001		
7. SL	Pearson's r	0.595 ***	0.863 ***	0.913 ***	0.823 ***	0.908 ***	0.859 ***	
	p-value	< .001	< .001	< .001	< .001	< .001	< .001	

Note. ***Correlation is statistically significant at $p < .001$.

Research Question Three

RQ3: Is there a difference in how officers perceive job satisfaction based on the years of service?

H_01 – There is no difference in officers' perceptions of job satisfaction regardless of the years of service.

H_{3a} There is a difference in how officers perceive job satisfaction based on the years of service.

The third research question assumes that perceptions of law enforcement officers differ in how they view servant leadership based on their years with the agency. The number of service years was categorized into four groups, and frequency statistics were used to describe the group breakdown: Group one is 1-5 years, Group two is 6-10 years, Group three is 11-15 years, and Group four is 16 or more years. A one-way ANOVA was conducted to examine whether officers perceived job satisfaction differently based on how many years they have served with the agency. The ANOVA indicated no statistically significant difference in job satisfaction between the four groups of tenure, F (3, 274) = .398, p = .755; therefore, no post hoc test was necessary because there were no differences to find.

The outcome between the four groups was non-significant, with groups one (M = 21.00, SD = 5.76), two (M = 21.17, SD = 5.84), three (M = 21.86, SD = 4.41), and four (M = 21.32, SD = 3.85) all showing similar results. See Table 4. These findings indicated that there were no significant differences in officers' perceptions of job satisfaction regardless of the years of service. The test assumptions were checked, and because of the large sample size (N = 278), the alpha level for Levene's test was set at p < .001. The Levene's equality of variance test was non-significant (p = .004), indicating that the assumption of homogeneity of variance was not violated. See Appendix A. Also, normality was checked with a Q-Q Plot, and no deviations were noted. See Figure 1 in Appendix A.

Table 4

Descriptives Statistics – Job Satisfaction and Years of Service

Years	N	Mean	SD	SE	Coefficient of variation
1-5 years	81	21.000	5.760	0.640	0.274
11-15 years	52	21.173	5.840	0.810	0.276
16+ years	68	21.868	4.411	0.535	0.202
6-10 years	77	21.325	3.857	0.440	0.181

Research Question Four

RQ4: Is there a difference in how officers perceive job satisfaction based on their level of education?

$H_0$1 – There is no difference in officers' perceptions of job satisfaction regardless of the levels of education.

H_{4a} – There is a difference in how officers perceive job satisfaction based on their level of education.

The fourth research question assumes that education does play a role in how officers perceive servant leadership and job satisfaction. Education was categorized into four levels, and frequency statistics were used to describe the four levels: level one - high school graduate (HS), level two - some college, level three - bachelor's degree (BA/BS), and level four - graduate degree (MA/MS). A one-way ANOVA was conducted to examine whether officers perceive job satisfaction differently based on their level of education. In other words, is there a difference among the four groups in how they perceive job satisfaction with formal education? The ANOVA indicated no statistically significant difference among the four education levels on job satisfaction, F (3, 274) = .141, p = .936; therefore, no post hoc test was conducted because there were no differences to find. The difference in perceptions between the four education levels was non-significant with levels one (M = 21.53, SD = 5.06), two (M = 21.34, SD – 4.83), three (M – 21.31, SD = 5.30), and four (M = 20.40, SD = 5.60) all having a similar outcome. See Table 5. These findings indicated that there were no significant differences in officers' perceptions of job satisfaction regardless of the levels of education. The test assumptions were checked with the alpha level for Levene's test set at p < .001. The Levene's equality of variance test was non-significant (p = .811), indicating that the assumption of homogeneity of variance was not violated. See

Appendix B. Also, normality was checked with a Q-Q Plot, and no deviations were noted. See

Figure 2 in Appendix B.

Table 5

Descriptives Statistics– Job Satisfaction and Education Levels

Education	N	Mean	SD	SE	Coefficient of variation
Bachelor's Degree	57	21.316	5.302	0.702	0.249
Graduate Degree	10	20.400	5.602	1.771	0.275
HS	45	21.533	5.066	0.755	0.235
Some College	166	21.343	4.838	0.375	0.227

Summary

Part Five discussed information on data collected from the participants and research setting

and analyses of the research questions. The data were collected using the OLA instrumentation by

surveying two law enforcement agencies (Laub, 1999), one from the Midwest and the other from

the Southwest region of the United States. Two agencies committed to the survey with 1,260

potential participants; the first agency employed 76 sworn personnel, including management, and

the second had 1,184 sworn personnel, including management. The response rate for Agency 1

and Agency 2 was 80% and 20%, respectively. This chapter contains the results from the four

research questions and ten hypotheses; the results from the analysis revealed statistically

significant correlations between servant leadership characteristics, size of the agency, and job

satisfaction. However, there were no differences in officers' perceptions of job satisfaction

regardless of tenure or education level. The researcher used descriptive statistics, ANOVA, and

correlational analyses to examine the data to determine the outcome of each hypothesis.

The findings supported eight of the ten hypotheses. The first eight hypotheses were

analyzed using Pearson's product-moment correlational analysis to examine the relationships between servant leadership characteristics and job satisfaction. The results indicated a statistically significant correlation between the six constructs of servant leadership characteristics and job satisfaction as measured by OLA. The ninth and tenth hypotheses were analyzed using a one-way ANOVA to examine the difference in officers' perceptions based on tenure and education demographics. The results did not support the hypotheses (H_{3a} and H_{4a}), which examined the relationships between job satisfaction, years of service, and education level. The ANOVA results indicated no statistically significant difference in job satisfaction regardless of tenure or education level. The next chapter, Chapter Five, presents the statistical results from Chapter Four. The chapter will discuss the practical assessment of the research questions, limitations of the study, and implications for future study.

PART SIX:
The Implications

The final section of this book is reserved for discussions and implications of the future of servant leadership. This research study focused on Robert Greenleaf's concept of servant leadership and its impact on organizational health and job satisfaction in law enforcement. The research concentrated on the ten principles of servant leadership: *listening, empathy, healing, awareness, persuasion, conceptualization, foresight, stewardship, commitment to growth, and building community* (Greenleaf, 1977). The Organizational Leadership Assessment (OLA), developed by Dr. Jim Laub (1999), was used to measure organizational health and job satisfaction. The study sought to examine the relationship between the characteristics of servant leadership and job satisfaction levels in law enforcement. Also under examination were demographics of tenure and education levels and whether the different levels affect the prevalence of job satisfaction. Two U.S. law enforcement agencies (Agency 1 from the Midwest and Agency 2 from the Southwest) were selected to participate in the research. The literature review in provided information on the success of servant leadership in various industries while identifying a gap in the literature on servant leadership and law enforcement. The preceding chapters reported the research results and corresponding data analyses.

This chapter aims to summarize, discuss, expand upon, and highlight the implications of the initial research assumptions presented in Part Two. The initial part of this chapter consists of a practical assessment of the study's research questions. Each research question will be analyzed, and additional findings, if any, will be presented. Further, the chapter will discuss the study's limitations and shortfalls during the research. Next, implications for future law enforcement leadership studies suggest exploring servant leadership and the ten servant leadership principles to improve job satisfaction, morale, and recruiting and retention. Finally, a summary of the research study will be presented to bring the research to a close.

Practical Assessment of Research Questions

This research examined servant leadership and its impact on job satisfaction in law enforcement. Law enforcement generally subscribes to an autocratic leadership style because of the nature of the job (e.g., situations are dynamic, option for deliberation is limited, and immediate decisions are necessary when public safety is at risk). However, and perhaps more critical, servant leadership has shown that when leaders prioritize serving, the byproduct is more efficient and productive employees (Blanchard, 2019; Greenleaf, 1977; Miao et al., 2014a). Moreover, contemporary challenges for law enforcement have shifted from focusing on militaristic tactics to personnel management and the ability to retain them. To this end, servant leadership or the ideals of servant leadership have become more attractive for promulgating positive morale, increasing work productivity and efficiency, and improving job satisfaction. Data on servant leadership and the impact on job satisfaction in law enforcement were collected and analyzed. The research questions that guided this study are as follows:

1. To what extent do characteristics of the six subscales of servant leadership behavior (values people, develops people, builds community, displays authenticity, provides leadership, shares leadership) correlate with the perceptions of police officers or deputy sheriffs regarding job satisfaction?

2. Is there a correlation between servant leadership and employee job satisfaction based on the agency size: (a) 50 or more officers or deputies but less than 500 and (b) 500 or more officers or deputies?

3. Is there a difference in how officers perceive job satisfaction based on their years of service?

4. Is there a difference in how officers perceive job satisfaction based on their levels of

education?

The researcher used descriptive statistics, one-way ANOVA, and correlational analyses to

examine the data in determining the outcome of each hypothesis. The findings supported eight of

the ten hypotheses. The first eight hypotheses were analyzed using Pearson's product-moment

correlational analysis to examine the relationships between servant leadership characteristics and

job satisfaction. The results indicated a statistically significant correlation between the six

constructs of servant leadership characteristics and job satisfaction as measured by OLA. The ninth

and tenth hypotheses were analyzed using a one-way ANOVA to examine the difference in

officers' perceptions based on the demographics of tenure and education. The results did not

support the hypotheses (H_{3a} and H_{4a}), which examined the relationships between job satisfaction,

years of service, and education levels. The ANOVA results indicated no statistically significant

difference in job satisfaction regardless of tenure or education level.

The study proceeded with solicitations of various U.S. law enforcement agencies to

participate in a survey study. Three law enforcement agencies were selected; however, the third

agency backed out due to a lack of leadership support. Of the two remaining agencies, one was

from the Midwest (Agency 1) and the other from the Southwest (Agency 2) region of the United

States. A total of 278 participants engaged in the survey study, with 55 from Agency 1 and 223

from Agency 2. Using correlation analysis, the first and second research questions examined the

six constructs of servant leadership and job satisfaction. The third and fourth questions applied a

one-way ANOVA to examine the differences; a demographic breakdown was provided for (1)

Service Years and (2) Education Levels.

Research Question One

The first research question examined the six constructs of servant leadership and how they correlate with job satisfaction in law enforcement. A Pearson's product-moment correlational analysis was conducted to examine how the six constructs correlated with job satisfaction. The researcher expected most if not all, constructs to have a strong correlation to job satisfaction because the constructs of servant leadership inculcate trust, which leads to autonomy, and the by-product is a more efficient and productive workforce (Eva et al., 2018; Joseph & Wilson, 2005; McGee-cooper et al., 2001). Further, Kiersch and Peters (2017) agreed that the six servant leadership constructs enrich followers' lives and positively impact employers and society. Moreover, Melinda and Antonio (2019) found high correlations between faculty morality and relationships in private and public universities—meaning, when faculties subscribe to servant leadership, students' experiences are enhanced, and they are more likely to be engaged.

Servant leadership has been found to enhance employee morale, increase productivity, and improve job satisfaction (Allen et al., 2018; Charles, 2015; Craun & Henson, 2022; Ebener, 2011; Ebener & O'Connell, 2010). The constructs of servant leadership, e.g., listening, empathy, foresight, and stewardship, to name a few, are well documented and explored (Crowther, 2015; Greenleaf, 1977; Spears, 1998). The purpose of servant leadership is to prioritize service first; in other words, putting the priority of others first. Bahmani et al. (2021) discovered that servant leaders expressed serving followers first rather than commanding them. Organizations that invest in servant leadership by fostering participatory decision-making, empowering, and nurturing enjoy much higher success, lower turnover, and a trusting environment (Thomas & Cangemi, 2021; Greenleaf, 1977; Russell, 2001). For a closer examination of each of the six constructs, the researcher analyzed the outcome from the tested hypotheses. The findings indicated that job satisfaction strongly correlated with the six constructs of servant leadership, which is consistent with prior research studies mentioned in the literature review in Chapter Two (Allen et al., 2018; Charles, 2015; Craun & Henson, 2022; Ebener, 2011; Ebener & O'Connell, 2010).

Research Question Two

Research Question Two examined the relationship between job satisfaction and the six constructs of servant leadership with two law enforcement agencies varying in size. In both agencies, the Organizational Leadership Assessment measured their job satisfaction level. The outcome of the correlation analysis found statistically significant relationships between job satisfaction and servant leadership at both agencies. However, in Agency 1, job satisfaction was more strongly related to the construction of *building community*. Whereas in Agency 2, job satisfaction was more strongly related to *valuing people*. The study revealed a consistently strong correlation between employees' perceptions of servant leadership characteristics (the six constructs) and job satisfaction. The differences in perceptions between Agency 1 and Agency 2 may be attributed to the different regions where law enforcement is practiced, their culture, values, or beliefs.

Prior studies on employee performance and job satisfaction yielded a strong correlation between the two variables, and improved performance is dependent on employee satisfaction (Eva et al., 2018; Joseph & Winston, 2005; Kiersch & Peters, 2017; Khuwaja et al., 2020; Yang et al., 2021). The organizations analyzed by the researcher in Chapter Two were of various professions from business, education, military, and religious groups. To be clear, however, while the types of organizations may differ, the desire for leadership and leading are consistent in all organizations— having the ability to influence others (Blanchard, 2019; Kouzes & Posner, 2012; Northouse, 2012;

Maxwell, 2007). Therefore, the types of organizations, services rendered, work environment, rules and regulations, and expectations may influence performance and job satisfaction differently.

While all six constructs of servant leadership revealed a strong correlation with job satisfaction, *displaying authenticity* generated the lowest score, whereas *building community* reflected the highest score for Agency 1. In Agency 2, the construct of *providing leadership* generated the lowest score, whereas *valuing people* reflected the highest score. The six constructs of servant leadership have salient implications for management, leadership, and organizations that value human performance. Laub (1999) indicates that the six constructs correlate highly with servant leadership. The OLA measures the six constructs essential to organizational health and leadership practices. For Agency 1, OLA revealed moderate to good organizational health; improving the constructs of *developing people* and *displaying authenticity* may increase positive perceptions of the organization. In sharp contrast, OLA revealed Agency 2 was in poor organizational health, with employees experiencing management as autocratic, characterized by low levels of trust, with the lowest key areas being the constructs of developing people and displaying *authenticity*. The current research findings are consistent with prior studies, which implicate servant leadership characteristics and job satisfaction exist (Bowman, 2005; Erkutlu & Chafra, 2015; Hays, 2008; Irving, 2005; Jennings & Stahl-Wert, 2016; Wheeler, 2012).

Research Question Three

Research Question Three explored how officers perceive job satisfaction based on tenure. The researcher assumes tenure plays a role in how officers perceive job satisfaction. Service years were categorized into four groups: Group One having 1-5 years, Group Two having 6-10 years, Group Three having 11-15 years, and Group Four having 16 or more years. A one-way ANOVA was performed, which indicated no statistically significant differences between the four demographic groups. The descriptive statistics coefficients for each group related to the third research question were as follows: Group One, 0.274; Group Two, 0.181; Group Three, 0.276; and Group Four, 0.202. These findings indicated no significant differences in officers' perceptions of job satisfaction regardless of the years of service. To be sure, after the one-way ANOVA yielded no statistically significant differences between the four groups, the test assumptions were checked using Levene's equality of variance test. The outcome of Levene's equality of variance test was not significant. A check for normality was also performed using the Q-Q Plot, and no deviations were noted.

The overall, non-statistically significant differences in job satisfaction between the four groups were not expected. However, servant leadership has been shown to increase work productivity and increase job satisfaction in most organizations (Allen et al., 2018; Charles, 2015; Craun & Henson, 2022; Ebener, 2011; Ebener & O'Connell, 2010). Typically, officers with 1-5 years of service are still learning the job and tend to be highly motivated to make a difference. This group of officers should have the highest job satisfaction among the four groups. The researcher expected Group One to have higher job satisfaction than Groups Two, Three, and Four. Whereas Group Four, officers with 16 or more years of service, are seasoned veterans and may tend to have a cynical approach, which could negatively impact job satisfaction. Job satisfaction in law enforcement is an understudied subject and should be further explored in future research.

Research Question Four

The fourth research question assumes that education does play a role in how officers perceive servant leadership and job satisfaction. The researcher assumes that individuals with formal education are more capable of critical thinking and, therefore, more readily recognize servant leadership principles. Servant leadership principles in education mean giving voice to the students, and teachers and students become joint inquirers, which leads to deeper insights and greater appreciation (Blanchard, 2019; Greenleaf, 1979; Hays, 2008; Knowles, 1978). For this study, education was categorized into four levels: Level One - high school graduate (HS); Level Two - some college; Level Three - bachelor's degree (BA/BS); and Level Four - graduate degree (MA/MS). A one-way ANOVA was conducted to examine whether officers perceive job satisfaction differently based on their levels of education. The ANOVA indicated no statistically significant differences between all education levels. Similar to the previous question, after the one-way ANOVA yielded no statistically significant differences between the different levels of education, the test assumptions were checked using Levene's equality of variance test. The outcome of Levene's equality of variance test was non-significant. A follow-up check for normality was also performed using the Q-Q Plot; no deviations were noted.

While servant leadership is an understudied topic in law enforcement, higher education institutions have embraced the concept and found a high correlation between faculty morality and relationships in private and public universities (Melinda & Antonio, 2019). Further, Erkutlu and Chafra (2015) found that when students trust their teachers, they are engaged and more inclined to express their opinions. The overall, non-statistically significant differences in job satisfaction with the levels of education in law enforcement were not predicted since nearly seventy-five percent of the respondents had only high school diplomas or some college. The surprise finding prompts a more profound investigation into whether education is a valued trait for law enforcement and whether education affects the prevalence of servant leadership.

Limitations of the Study

This research study aimed to investigate whether there is a correlation between servant leadership and job satisfaction in law enforcement. The researcher selected a quantitative methodology to assess law enforcement's servant leadership and job satisfaction. The OLA scale, developed by Laub (1999), was selected as the instrument of choice to collect and analyze the data for this research study. The data from the OLA survey was used to analyze the prevalence of job satisfaction based on six factors along with the six constructs of servant leadership. As a practicing leadership concept, servant leadership has not been extensively studied in law enforcement compared to other leadership paradigms, such as autocratic, transactional, and transformational leadership. Data from two law enforcement agencies were collected and analyzed using four research questions related to the research objectives. While the data yielded statistically significant results for the first two research questions, the third and fourth research questions indicated no statistically significant differences. In either case, the findings have some limitations.

The main limitation is that job satisfaction has not been empirically measured in law enforcement using the OLA instrument. The limited literature on servant leadership characteristics and employee job satisfaction in law enforcement challenged the researcher's decision to opt for a solo measuring instrument. To be clear, the OLA instrument has been validated, field tested in various organizations, and shown to have a strong correlation between the six constructs of servant leadership, organizational health, and job satisfaction (Laub, 1999). Furthermore, the statistical results from the OLA survey instrument provided salient data to validate the instrument's reliability in measuring organizational health in law enforcement. However, the researcher cautioned against generalization based on prior studies and findings of the correlation between servant leadership and job satisfaction. More research is necessary to draw a favorable inference regarding the relations between servant leadership and employee job satisfaction in law enforcement.

The penultimate limitation is that only two law enforcement agencies participated in the research study. There are about 18,000 law enforcement agencies in the United States, including federal, state, county, and municipal agencies (National Sources of Law Enforcement Employment Data, 2016). However, most agencies consist of only ten or fewer officers and, therefore, did not meet the criteria of this research study. Of those that did meet the research criteria, only two agencies were willing to participate in the survey study. Since the survey was limited to only two law enforcement agencies, the sampling, while meeting the University of Cumberland's criteria, may be insufficient to determine job satisfaction within the agencies. The limited sample may have affected the findings for one or more of the research questions and should not be generalized one way or the other.

The tertiary research limitation is that the OLA instrument alone may be insufficient in capturing employee job satisfaction. To be clear, the OLA instrument can assess organizational health and leadership. Furthermore, the instrument has been field-tested and validated as having high reliability and correlations with organizational performances and leadership (Laub, 1999). However, only six factors were used to assess job satisfaction versus the six constructs and sixty factors used to assess organizational health and leadership. While there were strong correlations between the OLA's six constructs of servant leadership and employee job satisfaction, future examination of law enforcement and job satisfaction may want to consider a secondary instrument along with the OLA instrument. Moreover, potentially asking more refined questions about whether education and years of experience affect how officers view job satisfaction may add depth to the research findings.

Implications for Future Study

This research study examined servant leadership in law enforcement and whether the prevalence of such leadership style improves job satisfaction. The study indicated a strong correlation between job satisfaction and the six constructs of servant leadership and supported Laub's (1999) claim that the OLA is a viable assessment instrument for servant leadership research. Furthermore, the data analyses suggested that servant leadership is valued in law enforcement as with other organizations and professions. Future research on this topic should include participant demographics and a larger sample size and consider additional assessment instruments along with the OLA for more comprehensive findings. First, including demographics in the study demonstrates an organization's diversity, equity, and inclusion practices. Second, expanding to different regions of the U.S. will increase the sample size and capture responses from the variation of law enforcement practices—culture, values, and beliefs. Third, using additional assessment tools as an accompaniment to OLA to assess employee job satisfaction specifically will produce more robust findings.

Summary

The study examined whether there is a correlation between the servant leadership behavior of law enforcement executives and employee job satisfaction. The findings of this research study suggest that servant leadership is a viable leadership style for developing future leaders. Servant leadership fosters an environment conducive to growth through a process of nurture and support, thus helping followers mature beyond what was initially thought possible (Blanchard, 2019; Greenleaf, 1977). However, the study does not suggest or advocate abandoning traditional leadership practices but rather incorporating servant leadership to promulgate trust, build confidence, and inculcate good citizenship by nurturing and supporting. Law enforcement has come under fire from politicians and citizens for excessive use of force, discriminatory practices, and unethical behaviors, further eroding public trust and support. The lack of support and harsh critiques from advocacy groups further deteriorated the profession's reputation; as a result, morale took a downward spiral, which impacted law enforcement's ability to recruit and retain officers and professional staff. Servant leadership in law enforcement is an emerging concept that supplements traditional leadership practices, such as autocratic, transactional, and transformational leadership styles. While most have heard of servant leadership, and others claim to have practiced servant leadership, few genuinely embody the art of servanthood. It is my hope that this research stimulates and sparks the interests of current and future leaders in law enforcement and that the information provided will give them a foundation for leading with a servant heart.

Bass (1985) and Burns (1978) suggested that autocratic leaders are favored and highly desired in military and paramilitary organizations because of the authority afforded to the leaders and the control of followers. However, not all situations call for an autocratic leadership response; depending on the circumstance, a softer paternal or servant approach may be more appropriate. Greenleaf (1978) and others (Blanchard, 2019; Kouzes & Posner, 2012; Maxwell, 2007) argued that followers must be nurtured and encouraged to grow through modeling, inspiring, and engaging consistently. Considering the current anti-law enforcement rhetoric and defunding the police movements pushing for police accountability and reform, a paradigm shift in leadership practice is warranted and necessary.

The study of servant leadership and its impact on organizations, leaders, and researchers is gaining popularity; however, very few studies have focused on law enforcement organizations, their leaders, and their members. This research examined servant leadership from two law enforcement organizations and whether the prevalence of servant leadership improved job satisfaction. The assessment instrument used to collect the data was the Organizational Leadership Assessment (OLA) developed by Laub (1999). The research instrument uses a 60-question survey to solicit perceptions of servant leadership with a Likert scale style rating of 1, strongly disagree, and 5, strongly agree. The OLA survey was designed to measure organizational health and leadership; Laub (1999) suggested that the survey could be used to measure people, a unit, or an entire organization. The study indicated a high correlation between the six constructs of servant leadership and employee job satisfaction at both agencies. Interestingly, the OLA indicated that Agency 1 was operating at moderate organizational health and Agency 2 at poor organizational health.

Law enforcement has changed, and so has the practice of leadership. What was once a white-male-dominated profession has evolved into a diverse community workforce. While some of the obstacles responsible for the considerable exodus of law enforcement officers are beyond the control of the leadership, for instance, financial challenges, governmental sanctions, and political rhetoric, many internal issues can be minimized or avoided. The approach focuses on the individual officers and ensures that their needs are met or that they are not further harmed. To this end, there are great opportunities for law enforcement leaders to explore servant leadership and its potential impact on the profession. As the advancement of technologies consumes the law enforcement profession and our workforce becomes younger and younger, leaders must embrace the changing climate and become servant leaders.

Definitions

Robert Greenleaf (1977) conceptualized servant leadership and ten characteristics that are the fundamental tenets of servant leaders. Key terms appear throughout this quantitative dissertation and are related to the different leadership styles and relevant terms relating to the target population. These terms are defined as follows:

Autocratic leadership: This style of leadership is arbitrary and controlling; the leaders make all the decisions without input, and they are concerned with task accomplishment rather than individuals (Bass & Stogdill, 1990; Northouse, 2012; Rast III et al., 2013; Van Vugt et al., 2004). However, when a crisis must be averted, rules must be followed, and time is not an option for decision-making, autocratic leaders are highly desirable (Bass, 1990; Fiaz et al., 2017).

Awareness: General awareness strengthens the leader, broadens perspectives, and "aids one in understanding issues involving ethics and values" (Spears, 1998, p. 6). Greenleaf (1977) suggests that when a leader is self-aware, there is more alertness and attention to the current situation, allowing the leader to retain more and contribute intuitive insights for the future.

Chief Officers: Chief officers, in this study, refer to executive-level personnel holding the rank of Commander, Assistant Chiefs, Chiefs, Under Sheriffs, and Sheriffs. In some cases, the rank of Captain and Lieutenant are also considered executive leaders.

Commitment to Growth: Servant leaders put others as a priority over self. "The servant-leader is deeply committed to the growth of each and every individual within his or her institution" (Spears, 1998, p. 7).

Community: Community in the context of servant leadership is team building. Spears (1998) suggests that servant leaders should identify means to build community with those in businesses and other organizations. Moreover, building community inspires and lifts individuals up and helps them achieve more; Greenleaf (1977) said, "All that is needed to rebuild community as a viable life form for large enough numbers of people is for enough servant-leaders to show the way" (p. 39).

Conceptualization: Servant leaders think beyond the day-to-day operation; they conceptualize futuristic goals for long-term sustainability (Spears, 1998). In comparison, a leader who is an operator is primarily concerned with the day-to-day tasks and getting things done. In contrast, a conceptualizing leader is "concerned with what ought to be done—when, how, at what cost, in what priority, and how well it was done" (Greenleaf, 1977, p. 67).

Democratic leadership: This leadership style treats followers as equal and capable performers— leaders and followers make decisions together. Northouse (2012) suggests that "Democratic leaders do not use 'top-down' communication; instead, they speak on the same level as their subordinates" (p. 56).

Empathy: A servant leader has deep concerns for others; he always accepts and empathizes with others (Greenleaf, 1977; Northouse, 2012; Spears, 1998). A servant leader understands and values the uniqueness of individuals; Spears (1998) puts it this way, "One assumes the good intentions of co-workers and does not reject them as people" (p. 5). Greenleaf (1977) further asserts that followers achieve more when leaders empathize and accept them for who they are as individuals.

Foresight: Foresight is the ability to envision future solutions based on lessons learned from the past and what is being done currently. Greenleaf (1977) describes it as a constant analysis of events that allows leaders to project future outcomes. Spears (1998) asserts that "Foresight is a characteristic that enables the servant-leader to understand the lessons from the past, the realities of the present, and the likely consequences of a decision for the future" (p. 7).

Healing: In the context of servant leadership, healing refers to the need to be mentally and emotionally well so the leader can connect with others. Servant leaders acknowledge the complexities of humans and the challenges people face—spiritually and emotionally—and they "recognize that they have an opportunity to 'help make whole' those with whom they come in contact" (Spears, 1998, p. 6).

Law Enforcement: This is an all-encompassing term denoting those with authority to enforce federal, state, and municipal statutes. For the purpose of this study, law enforcement refers to police and sheriff's agencies.

Listening: Listening skills are necessary for all leaders for communication and decision-making. Listening helps clarify the needs and will of followers, and it is one of the most important ways to respond to followers (Northouse, 2012; Spears, 1998). Greenleaf (1977) puts it this way, "a true natural servant automatically responds to any problem by listening first" (p. 17).

Persuasion: Persuasion is one of the key tenets of servant leadership; having the ability to persuade compliance over coercion builds trust and strengthens relationships. Spears (1998) asserts, "The servant-leader seeks to convince others rather than coerce compliance" (p. 6). One of the ways to effectively persuade followers is to convince one person at a time (Greenleaf, 1977).

Police Officers: Police officers are equivalent to line employees and are either assigned to uniform assignment, plainclothes, or administrative tasks as required by the agency. Police officers must complete a rigorous training police academy, which meets or exceeds state and federal statutes, before being sworn in as police officers.

Public Safety: Public safety refers to law enforcement as defined previously.

Stewardship: Servant leaders are good stewardesses of followers and the organizations; stewards "assume first and foremost a commitment to serving the needs of others" (Spears, 1998, p.7).

Servant leaders advocate for their followers, ensuring everyone has the opportunities to achieve higher goals; servant leaders are "those who stand outside but are intimately concerned, and who, with the benefit of some detachment, oversee the active leaders" (p. 40).

Sworn Officers: Sworn officers in this context refer to all law enforcement personnel—police and sheriffs—that have completed the required training and have been sworn in by a public official, typically the Chief or the Sheriff. Sworn officers have the authority to effect an arrest, issue citations, prepare criminal investigations, and all the powers of a peace officer granted by the state.

Transactional leadership: "Transactional leadership occurs when one person takes the initiative in making contact with others for the purpose of an exchange of something valued" (Kuhnert & Lewis, 1987, p. 648). Essentially, transactional leaders engage followers in a mutual relationship where both individuals benefit; Yukl (1981) suggests it is a relationship of mutual dependence where leaders and followers acknowledge the contribution as well as rewards.

Transformational leadership: This leadership style suggests leaders elevate followers by raising their levels of awareness so followers may achieve more than originally thought possible (Bass, 1990). Transformational leadership has four components: intellectual stimulation, individual consideration, inspirational motivation, and idealized influence. Transformational leaders with the four qualities are suitable for organizations because of their ability to foster team dynamics, envision organizational effectiveness, and inspire trust in followers (Burns, 1978; Long et al., 2014).

List of Tables

List of Figures

References

Aboramadan, M., Dahleez, K., & Hamad, M. (2020). Servant leadership and academics' engagement in higher education: mediation analysis. *Journal of Higher Education Policy and Management, 42*(6), 617–633. https://doi.org/10.1080/1360080X.2020.1774036

Akins, R. B., Tolson, H., & Cole, B. R. (2005). Stability of response characteristics of a Delphi panel: application of bootstrap data expansion. *BMC Medical Research Methodology, 5*(1), 1-12.

Allen, S., Winston, B. E., Tatone, G. R., & Crowson, H. M. (2018). Exploring a model of servant leadership, empowerment, and commitment in nonprofit organizations. *Nonprofit Management and Leadership, 29*(1), 123–140. https://doi.org/10.1002/nml.21311

Amey, M. J. (2006). Leadership in higher education. *Change: The magazine of higher learning, 38*(6), 55-58.

Andersen, J. (2009). When a servant leader comes knocking …. *Leadership & Organization Development Journal, 30*(1), 4–15. https://doi.org/10.1108/01437730910927070

Armacost, B. E. (2004). Organizational culture and police misconduct. *George Washington Law Review, 72(3),* 453-546.

Badger, J. (2017). *The influence of servant leadership on subordinate resilience in law enforcement.* ProQuest Dissertations Publishing.

Bahmani, E., Teimouri, H., Moshref Javadi, M. H., & Rabbani Khorasegani, A. (2021). Theoretical development of servant leadership in a military context: A mixed methods research. *Human Systems Management, 40*(1), 65–80. https://doi.org/10.3233/HSM-200936

Baker, D. (2020). *Cultivating community-focused norms in law enforcement: servant leadership, accountability systems, and officer attitudes.* ProQuest dissertations publishing.

Banks, D., Hendrix, J., Hickman, M., & Kyckelhahn, T. (2016). *National sources of law nforcement employment data.* Ojp.gov. https://bjs.ojp.gov/content/pub/pdf/nsleed.pdfBarbuto, J. E., & Wheeler, D. W. (2006). Scale development and construct clarification of servant leadership. *Group and Organization Management,* *31*(3), 300–326. https://doi.org/10.1177/1059601106287091.

Bass, B. M. (1985). *Leadership and performance beyond expectations.* Free Press

Bass, B. M. (1990). From transactional to transformational leadership: Learning to share the vision. *Organizational Dynamics, 18*(3), 19–31. https://doi.org/10.1016/0090-2616(90)90061-S

Bass, B. M., & Avolio, B. J. (1990). Developing transformational leadership: 1992 and beyond. *Journal of European industrial training.*

Bass, B. M., & Bass, R. (2009). *The Bass handbook of leadership: Theory, research, and managerial applications.* Free Press.

Bass, B. M., & Stogdill, R. M. (1990). *Bass & Stogdill's handbook of leadership: Theory, research, and managerial applications.* Simon and Schuster.

Berger, A. (1996). *Research made simple: A handbook for the human services.* SAGE.

Berry, T. R. (2015). Servant leadership as an institutionalized model in Air Force education. *Journal of Education and Human Development,* *4*(2), 123–129. https://doi.org/10.15640/jehd.v4n2a14

Birch, B. C. (2002). Leadership as stewardship. *Quarterly Review: A Journal of Theological Resources for Ministry, 22*(4), 358-369.

Blanchard, K. (2019). *Leading at a higher level.* 3rd ed. Pearson Education.

Block, P. (2013). *Stewardship: Choosing service over self-interest.* Berrett-Koehler Publishers.

Bowman, R. F. (2005). Teacher as Servant Leader. *The Clearing House: A Journal of Educational Strategies, Issues and Ideas*, *78*(6), 257–260. https://doi.org/10.3200/tchs.78.6.257-260

Bradley, Y. (1999). Servant Leadership: A critique of Robert Greenleaf's concept of leadership. *Journal of Christian Education*, (2), 43-54.

Brown, M. & Hale, K. (2014). *Applied research methods in public and nonprofit organizations*. John Wiley & Sons.

Burkhardt, J. & Joslin, J. (Ed.). (2020). *Inspiration for servant-leaders: Lessons from fifty years of research and practice.* Greenleaf center for servant leadership.

Burns, J. M. (1978). *Leadership.* Harper & Row.

Burns, J. M. (2012). *Leadership.* Open Road Media.

Camp, N. P., Voigt, R., Jurafsky, D., & Eberhardt, J. L. (2021). The thin blue waveform: Racial disparities in officer prosody undermine institutional trust in the police. *Journal of Personality and Social Psychology*, *121*(6), 1157–1171. https://doi.org/10.1037/pspa0000270.supp (Supplemental)

Camm, T. W. (2019). The dark side of servant leadership. *13*, 107–132.

Charles, D. (2015). Effects of servant leadership on satisfaction with leaders: Inclusion of situational variables. *Emerging Leadership Journeys*, *8*(1), 46–62.

Chen, Z., Zhu, J., & Zhou, M. (2015). How does a servant leader fuel the service fire? A multilevel model of servant leadership, individual self-identity, group competition climate, and customer service performance. *Journal of Applied Psychology*, *100*(2), 511.

Chief of police demographics and statistics (2022). Number of chiefs of police in the US. (2022, September 9). Zippia.com. https://www.zippia.com/chief-of-police-jobs/demographics/?survey_step=step3

Coggins, E., & Bocarnea, M. C. (2015). The impact of servant leadership to followers' psychological capital: a comparative study of evangelical Christian leader-follower relationships in the United States and Cambodia. *Journal of Leadership, Accountability and Ethics, 12*(4), 111–144.

Cordner, G. (1978). Open and closed models of police organizations: traditions, dilemmas, and practical considerations. *Journal of Police Science and Administration, 6*(1), 22-34.

Craun, J. R., & Henson, J. D. (2022). Transitioning to a servant leadership culture through the teachings of Jesus. *European Journal of Theology and Philosophy, 2*(2), 1–8. https://doi.org/10.24018/theology.2022.2.2.61

Creswell, J. & Creswell, J. (2018). *Research design: Qualitative, quantitative, and mixed methods approaches.* 5th ed. Sage.

Crowther, S. (2018). *Biblical servant leadership: An exploration of leadership for the contemporary context.* Palgrave Macmillan Cham.

DeAngelis, R. T. (2021). Systemic Racism in Police Killings: New Evidence From the Mapping Police Violence Database, 2013–2021. *Race and Justice*, 21533687211047943.

Deluga, R. J., & Souza, J. (1991). The effects of transformational and transactional leadership styles on the influencing behaviour of subordinate police officers. *Journal of Occupational Psychology, 64*(1), 49-55.

Dennis, R. S., & Bocarnea, M. (2005). Development of the servant leadership assessment Instrument. *Leadership and Organization Development Journal, 25*(8), 600-615.

Depree, M. (1989). *Leadership is an art.* Doubleday.

DePree, M. (2002). Servant-leadership: Three things necessary. *Focus on leadership: Servant leadership for the, 21*, 89-100.

Diebels, K. J., Leary, M. R., & Chon, D. (2018). Individual differences in selfishness as a major dimension of personality: A reinterpretation of the sixth personality factor. *Review of General Psychology, 22*(4), 367–376. https://doi.org/10.1037/gpr0000155

Dimock, M. (2010, March 25). *About.* Pew Research Center. https://www.pewresearch.org/about/

Dubois, D., Rucker, D. D., & Galinsky, A. D. (2015). Social class, power, and selfishness: When and why upper and lower class individuals behave unethically. *Journal of Personality and Social Psychology, 108*(3), 436–449. https://doi.org/10.1037/pspi0000008

Duret, D. & Li, W. (2023). It's not just a police problem. Americans are opting out of government Jobs. The Marshall Project. https://www.themarshallproject.org/2023/01/21/ police-hiring-government-jobs-decline.

Earnhardt, M. P. (2008). Testing a servant leadership theory among United States military members. *Emerging Leadership Journeys, 1*(2), 14–24.

Ebener, D. R. (2011). Servant leadership and a culture of stewardship. *Priest, 67*(February), 17–21.

Ebener, D. R., & O'Connell, D. (2010). How might servant leadership work? *Nonprofit Management and Leadership, 20*(4), 83–96. https://doi.org/10.1002/nml

Enter, J. E. (2006). *Challenging the law enforcement organization: The road to effective leadership.* Narrow Road Press.

Erkutlu, H., & Chafra, J. (2015). Servant leadership and voice behavior in higher education. *Hacettepe University Journal of Education, 30*(4), 29-41.

Eva, N., Sendjaya, S., Prajogo, D., Cavanagh, A., & Robin, M. (2018). Creating strategic fit: Aligning servant leadership with organizational structure and strategy. *Personnel Review, 47*(1), 166–186. https://doi.org/10.1108/PR-03-2016-0064

Faul, F., Erdfelder, E., Lang, A. G., & Buchner, A. (2007). G* Power 3: A flexible statistical power analysis program for the social, behavioral, and biomedical sciences. *Behavior research methods, 39*(2), 175-191.

Fatima, T., Majeed, M., Jahanzeb, S., Gul, S., & Irshad, M. (2021). Servant leadership and machiavellian followers: A moderated mediation model. *Journal of Work and Organizational Psychology, 37*, 215–229.

Fiaz, M., Qin Su, Ikram, A., & Saqib, A. (2017). Leadership styles and employees' motivation: a perspective from an emerging economy. *Journal of Developing Areas, 51*(4), 143–156. https://doi.org/10.1353/jda.2017.0093

Fleenor, J. W. (2006). Trait approach to leadership. *Psychology, 37*(1), 651-665.

Force, P. (2003). *Self-interest before Adam Smith: A genealogy of economic science.* Vol. 68. Cambridge University Press.

Fry, L. W., Matherly, L. L., Whittington, J. L., & Winston, B. E. (2007). Spiritual leadership as an integrating paradigm for servant leadership. *Integrating spirituality and organizational leadership*, 70-82.

Gibson, R., O'Leary, K., & Weintraub, J. (2020). The little things that make employees feel appreciated. Harvard Business Review. https://hbr.org/2020/01/the-little-things-that-make-employees-feel-appreciated

Girden, E. R., & Kabacoff, R. (Eds.). (2010). *Evaluating research articles from start to finish.* Sage.

Graduate School Doctoral, (2022). University of the Cumberlands, doctoral research handbook.

Greenblatt, A. (August 14, 2020). Police chiefs most open to reform are the ones leaving. Governing. https://www.governing.com/now/police-chiefs-most-open-to-reform-are-the-ones-leaving.html

Greenleaf, R. (1977). *Servant leadership.* A journey into the nature of legitimate power and greatness. Paulist Press.

Greenleaf, R. (1998). *The power of servant-leadership: Essays.* Berrett-Koehler Publishers.

Harms, P. D., & Spain, S. M. (2015). Beyond the bright side: Dark personality at work. *Applied Psychology, 64*(1), 15–24. https://doi.org/10.1111/apps.12042

Hays, J. (2008). "Teacher as servant: Applications of Greenleaf's servant leadership in higher Education." *Journal of Global Business Issues,* Vol. 2 No. 1, pp. 113.

Hendriks, F., & Karsten, N. (2014). Theory of democratic leadership. *P.'t Hart & R. Rhodes (Eds.), Oxford handbook of political leadership*, 41-56.

Heyler, S. G., & Martin, J. A. (2018). Servant leadership theory: Opportunities for additional theoretical integration. *Journal of Managerial Issues*, 230-243.

Hutapea, B. (2022). Servant leadership among higher education academic leaders: the role of personality traits. *Proceedings of the 3rd Tarumanagara International Conference on the Applications of Social Sciences and Humanities (TICASH 2021), 655*(Ticash 2021), 1762–1768. https://doi.org/10.2991/assehr.k.220404.286

Iken, S. L. (2005). *Servant leadership in higher education: Exploring perceptions of educators and staff employed in a university setting*. The University of North Dakota.

Irving, J. A. (2005). Servant leadership and the effectiveness of teams. Regent University.

Jackson & Lee, P. C. (2019). Servant leadership in times of crisis: Southeastern Virginia Police Chiefs respond. S.A.M. *Advanced Management Journal (1984), 84*(4), 22–.

JASP Team (2023). JASP (Version 0.17.1)[Computer software].

Jennings, K., & Stahl-Wert, J. (2016). *The serving leader: Five powerful actions to transform your team, business, and community*. Berrett-Koehler Publishers.

Jermier, J. M., & Berkes, L. J. (1979). Leader behavior in a police command bureaucracy: A closer look at the quasi-military model. *Administrative Science Quarterly*, 1-23.

Jobs. (n.d.). International Association of Chiefs of Police. Retrieved July 26, 2023, from https://www.theiacp.org/jobs

Jonason, P. K., & Webster, G. D. (2010). The dirty dozen: A concise measure of the dark triad. *Psychological Assessment*, *22*(2), 420–432. https://doi.org/10.1037/a0019265

Joseph, E. E., & Winston, B. E. (2005). A correlation of servant leadership, leader trust, and organizational trust. *Leadership & Organization Development Journal*.

Khuwaja, U., Ahmed, K., Abid, G., & Adeel, A. (2020). Leadership and employee attitudes: The mediating role of perception of organizational politics. *Cogent Business and Management*, *7*(1), 1–21. https://doi.org/10.1080/23311975.2020.1720066

Kiersch, C., & Peters, J. (2017). Leadership from the inside out: student leadership development within authentic leadership and servant leadership frameworks. *Journal of Leadership Education*, *16*(1), 148–168. https://doi.org/10.12806/v16/i1/t4

Kirkpatrick, S. A., & Locke, E. A. (1996). Direct and indirect effects of three-charismatic leadership components on performance and attitudes. *Journal of Applied Psychology, 81*(1), 36-51.

Knowles, M. S. (1978). Andragogy: Adult learning theory in perspective. *Community College Review, 5*(3), 9-20.

Knowles, M. S., Holton, I. E. F., & Swanson, R. A. (2005). *The adult learner: The definitive classic in adult education and human resource development*. Taylor & Francis Group.

Koehler, J. W., & Pankowski, J. (1997). *Transformational leadership in government*. Lucie Press.

Kotter, J. (2012). *Leading change*. Harvard Business Review.

Kouzes, J. & Posner, B. (2012). *The leadership challenge: How to make extraordinary things happen in organizations.* 5th ed. 25th anniversary. Wiley

Kuhnert, K. W., & Lewis, P. (1987). Transactional and transformational leadership: A constructive/developmental analysis. *Academy of Management Review, 12*(4), 648-657.

Ladkin, D., & Taylor, S. S. (2010). Leadership as art: Variations on a theme. *Leadership, 6*(3), 235-241.

Laub, J. A. (1999). *Assessing the servant organization: Development of the servant organizational leadership assessment (SOLA) instrument*. Florida Atlantic University.

Laub, J. A. (2000). *Development of the organizational leadership assessment (OLA) instrument*.

Lee, J. A. (1977). Leader power for managing change. *Academy of Management Review, 2*(1), 73-80.

Lee, A., Lyubovnikova, J., Tian, A. W., & Knight, C. (2020). Servant leadership: A meta-analytic examination of incremental contribution, moderation, and mediation. *Journal of Occupational and Organizational Psychology*, *93*(1), 1-44.

Li, W., & Mahajan, I. (Originally published: September 1, 2021). American police say officers are quitting in droves. Federal data says otherwise. *Time*. https://time.com/6093684/police-quitting-federal-data/

Liden, R. C., Wayne, S. J., Zhao, H., & Henderson, D. (2008). Servant leadership: Development of a multidimensional measure and multi-level assessment. *The Leadership Quarterly*, *19*(2), 161-177.

Liden, R. C., Wayne, S. J., Liao, C., & Meuser, J. D. (2014). Servant leadership & serving culture. *Academy of Management Journal*, *57*(5), 1434–1452.

Long, C. S., Yusof, W. M. M., Kowang, T. O., & Heng, L. H. (2014). The impact of transformational leadership style on job satisfaction. *World Applied Sciences Journal*, *29*(1), 117-124.

Locke, L. (2019). The clay feet of servant leadership. *Journal of Biblical Integration in Business*, *22*(1), 34–42.

Maloş, R. (2012). Leadership styles. *Annals of Eftimie Murgu University Resita, Fascicle II, Economic Studies*.

Mason, R. (2016). The recognition gap: Hourly employees want more recognition. Recognition and engagement excellence essentials. https://www.proquest.com/magazines/recognition-gap-hourly-employees-want-more/docview/1954904927/se-2

Maxwell, J. (2007). *The 21 irrefutable laws of leadership.* Harper Collins.

McCann, J. T., Graves, D., & Cox, L. (2014). Servant leadership, employee satisfaction, and organizational performance in rural community hospitals. *International Journal of Business and Management, 9*(10), 28.

McDevitt, J. (2009). Political influences on racial disparities in traffic enforcement practices. *Criminology & public policy, 8*(2), 337–341. https://doi.org/10.1111/j.1745-9133.2009.00568.x

McGee-Cooper, A., & Looper, G. (2001). *The essentials of servant-leadership: Principles in practice*. Dallas: Pegasus Communications.

McGinty, J. (n.d.). *Chapter 2*. Policeforum.org. https://www.policeforum.org/chapter2

Melinda, T. & Antonio, T. (2019, October). Servant leadership dimension in higher education. In *2019 International Conference on Organizational Innovation (ICOI 2019)* (pp. 677-681). Atlantis Press.

Miao, Q., Newman, A., Schwarz, G., & Xu, L. (2014a). Servant leadership, trust, and the organizational commitment of public sector employees in China. *Public Administration, 92*(3), 727–743. https://doi.org/10.1111/padm.12091

Miao, Q., Newman, A., Schwarz, G., & Xu, L. I. N. (2014b). Servant leadership, trust, and the organizational commitment of public sector employees in China. *92*(3). https://doi.org/10.1111/padm.12091

Mitchell, T. (2017, January 11). *2. Inside America's police departments*. Pew Research Center's Social & Demographic Trends Project. https://www.pewresearch.org/social-trends/2017/01/11/inside-americas-police-departments/

Moore, M. (1976). A 'normative' model for law enforcement in the criminal justice system. *Journal of Police Science and Administration, 4*(1), 71-81.

Morabito, M., & Shelley, T. O. C. (2015). Representative bureaucracy: Understanding the correlates of the lagging progress of diversity in policing. *Race and Justice, 5*(4), 330-355.

Morin, R. (2017, January 11). *Behind the badge.* Pew Research Center's Social & Demographic Trends Project. https://www.pewresearch.org/social-trends/2017/01/11/behind-the-badge/

Murray, T. (2000). Police and the challenge of the 21st century: managing change in police organizations. *Platypus Magazine*, (68).

National Sources of Law. (2016). U.S. Department of Justice. Office of Justice Programs. Bureau of Justice Statistics. https://bjs.ojp.gov/content/pub/pdf/nsleed.pdf

Northouse, P. (2012). *Leadership: Theory and practice.* 7th ed. Sage.

Ortmeier, P. J., & Meese, E. (2010). *Leadership, ethics, and policing: Challenges for the 21st century.* Prentice Hall.

Palumbo, R. (2016). Challenging servant leadership in the nonprofit sector. *6*(2), 81–98.

Patterson, K. A. (2003). *Servant leadership: A theoretical model.* Regent University.

Phillips, D. C., & Burbules, N. C. (2000). *Postpositivism and educational research.* Rowman & Littlefield.

Police Chiefs Compensation. (n.d.). Policeforum.org. PERF 2021 Survey https://www.policeforum.org/assets/ChiefsCompensation.pdf

Police Chief Magazine, (n.d.). A crisis facing the law. *No title.* (n.d.). Policechiefmagazine.org. https://www.policechiefmagazine.org/a-crisis-facing-law-enforcement-recruiting-in-the-21st-century/

Premeaux, S., & Bedeian, A. (2015). Self-monitoring. In *Encyclopedia of Psychopharmacology* (pp. 1543–1543). https://doi.org/10.1007/978-3-642-36172-2_200715.

Racaj, M., & Gelev, I. (2015). Leadership in military operations. *Contemporary Macedonian Defence–International Scientific Defence, Security and Peace Journal*, *15*(28), 59-68.

Rast III, D., Hogg, M., & Giessner, S. (2013). Self-uncertainty and Support for Autocratic Leadership. *Self & Identity*, *12*(6), 635–649. https://doi.org/10.1080/15298868.2012.718864

Reaves, B. (2015). Ojp.gov. https://bjs.ojp.gov/content/pub/pdf/lpd13ppp.pdf

Roberts, R. (2018). Twelve principles of modern military leadership. *NCO Journal*, 1-8.

Russell, R. F. (2001). The role of values in servant leadership. *Leadership & Organization Development Journal*, *22*(2), 76–84. https://doi.org/10.1108/01437730110382631

Sendjaya, S., & Sarros, J. C. (2002). Servant leadership: Its origin, development, and application in organizations. *Journal of Leadership & Organizational Studies*, *9*(2), 57-64.

Sendjaya, S. (2005). Morality and leadership: Examining the ethics of transformational leadership. *Journal of Academic Ethics*, *3*(1), 75-86.

Shim, H. S., Jo, Y., & Hoover, L. T. (2015). Police transformational leadership and organizational commitment: Mediating role of organizational culture. *Policing*, *38*(4), 754–774. https://doi.org/10.1108/PIJPSM-05-2015-0066

Shim, Park, H. H., & Eom, T. H. (2016). Public servant leadership: Myth or powerful reality? *International Review of Public Administration*, *21*(1), 3–20. https://doi.org/10.1080/12294659.2016.1147753

Shults, J. (December 15, 2022). What officers said were the biggest challenges of 2022 (and why leaders should pay attention). https://www.police1.com/2022-year-review/articles/what-officers-said-were-the-biggest-challenges-of-2022-and-why-leaders-should-pay-attention-5sKfxYONpjZMmmS6/

Sklansky, D. A. (2005). Not your father's police department: Making sense of the new demographics of law enforcement. *J. Crim. L. & Criminology*, *96*, 1209.

Spatz, C. (2019). *Exploring statistics: Tales of distribution*. 12th ed. Outcrop Publisher.

Spears, L. (Ed.). (1998). *The power of servant leadership.* Berrett-Koehler.

Spears, L. C. (2010). Character and servant leadership: Ten characteristics of effective, caring leaders. *The journal of virtues & leadership*, *1*(1), 25-30.

Stone, A. G., Russell, R. F., & Patterson, K. (2004). Transformational versus servant leadership: A difference in leader focus. *Leadership & Organization Development Journal*, *25*(4), 349-361.

Thomas, A., & Cangemi, J. (2021). Authoritarian, transactional, and transformational Leadership styles in law enforcement. *Organization Development Journal*, *39*(1), 33-44.

Turner, J. C., & Hamstra, C. (2018). *Servant Leadership in the Military*. iUniverse.

van Dierendonck, D. (2011). Servant leadership: A review and synthesis. *Journal of Management*, *37*(4), 1228–1261. https://doi.org/10.1177/0149206310380462

van Dierendonck, D., & Nuijten, I. (2011). The servant leadership survey: development and validation of a multidimensional measure. *Journal of Business and Psychology*, *26*(3), 249–267. https://doi.org/10.1007/s10869-010-9194-1

Van Vugt, M., Jepson, S. F., Hart, C. M., & De Cremer, D. (2004). Autocratic leadership in social dilemmas: A threat to group stability. *Journal of Experimental Social Psychology*, *40*(1), 1-13.

Washington, R., Sutton, C., & Feild, H. (2006). Individual differences in servant leadership: The roles of values and personality. *Leadership & Organization Development Journal*, *27*(8), 700-716.

Wheeler, D. W. (2012). *Servant leadership for higher education: Principles and practices*. John Wiley & Sons.

Wiley, C. (1993). The incentive plan pushes production. *Workforce Management, 72*(8), 86–.

Winston, B. E., & Patterson, K. (2006). An integrative definition of leadership. *International Journal of Leadership Studies, 1*(2), 6–66.

Wisse, B., & Sleebos, E. (2016). When the dark ones gain power: perceived position power strengthens the effect of supervisor Machiavellianism on abusive supervision in work teams. *Critical studies on security, 2*(2), 210–222.

WorkforceSurvey *June 2021.* (n.d.). Policeforum.org. https://www.policeforum.org/workforcesurveyjune2021

Yang, C., Zhang, W., Wu, S., Kee, D. M. H., Liu, P., & Deng, H. (2021). Influence of chief executive officer servant leadership on middle managers' voice behavior. *Social Behavior and Personality: an international journal, 49*(5), 1-13.

Yu, X. (2011). Theory of humans: Selfishness. *Available at SSRN 1974395.*

Yukl, G. (1981). *Leadership in Organizations, 9/e.* Pearson Education India.

Yukl, G. (2012). Effective leadership behavior: What we know and what questions need more attention. Academy of Management Perspectives, 26(4), 66-85.

Zane, M. (2023, January 30). *What is the Working Age population in the U.S.? [2023]: Statistics on prime Working Age population in America.* Zippia. https://www.zippia.com/advice/working-age-population/

Appendix A

Job Satisfaction and Years of Service (RQ3)

Test for Equality of Variances (Levene's)

F	df1	df2	p
4.617	3.000	274.000	0.004

Figure 1

Q-Q Plot

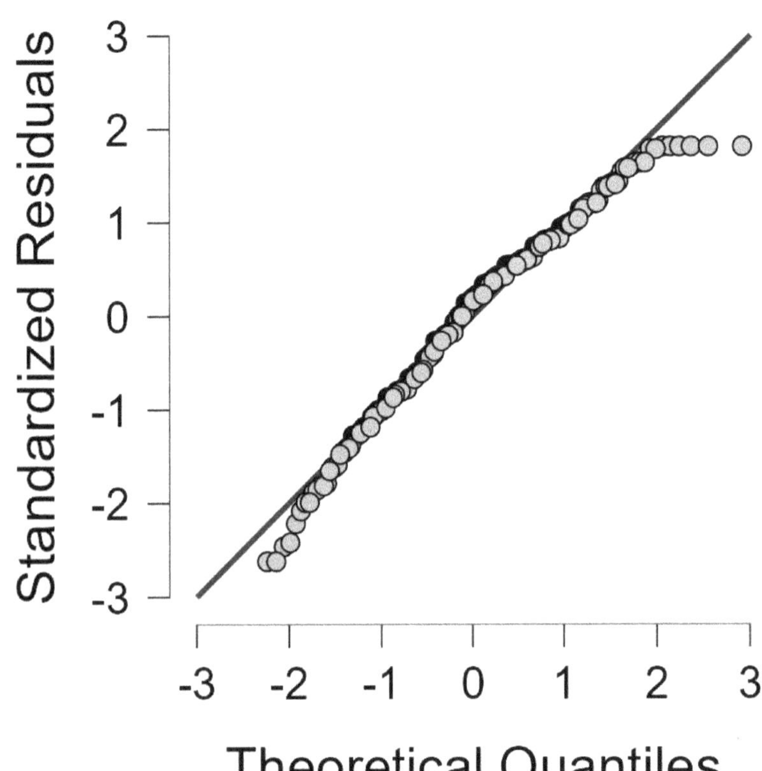

Appendix B

Job Satisfaction and Education Levels (RQ4)

Test for Equality of Variances (Levene's)

F	df1	df2	p
0.319	3.000	274.000	0.811

Figure 2

Q-Q Plot

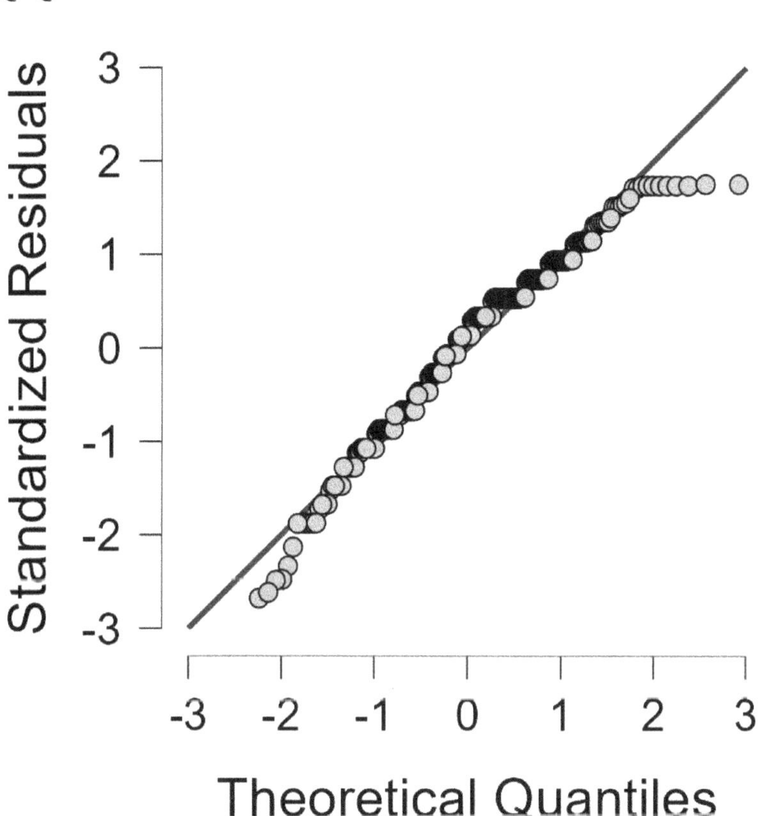

THE ALLEN COUNTY COURTHOUSE
715 CALHOUN ST, FORT WAYNE, IN 46802

FORT WAYNE OUTFITTERS, 1004 CASS ST, FORT WAYNE, IN 46808

PROMENADE PARK, 202 W SUPERIOR ST, FORT WAYNE, IN 46802

CLUB SODA
235 E SUPERIOR ST, FORT WAYNE, IN 46802

THE WELLS STREET BRIDGE
N WELLS ST, FORT WAYNE, IN 46802

THE SPIRIT OF FORT WAYNE, PUFFERBELLY JUNCTION

PROMENADE PARK, 202 W SUPERIOR ST, FORT WAYNE, IN 46802

WELCOME MURAL, HARRISON STREET

THE ALLEY
816 PINT N SLICE, FORT WAYNE, IN 46802

GNOMETOWN BREWING COMPANY, 118 W COLUMBIA ST
FORT WAYNE, IN 46802

HARRISON UNDERPASS

PENNY DRIP
815 LAFAYETTE ST, FORT WAYNE, IN 46802

HONEY PLANT
1436 N WELLS ST, FORT WAYNE, IN 46808

MARQUEE AT THE LANDING
131 W COLUMBIA ST, FORT WAYNE, IN 46802

THE RIVERFRONT AT PROMENADE PARK
124 W SUPERIOR ST, FORT WAYNE, IN 46802

PROMENADE PARK
202 W SUPERIOR ST, FORT WAYNE, IN 46802

SHARON'S VICTORIAN HOUSE & GIFTS
634 W BERRY ST, FORT WAYNE, IN 46802

MERCADO, 111 W COLUMBIS ST, FORT WAYNE, IN 46802

MERCADO, 111 W COLUMBIS ST, FORT WAYNE, IN 46802

MERCADO, 111 W COLUMBIS ST, FORT WAYNE, IN 46802

WAYNE MILLS KNITTING PARK
623 WATKINS ST, FORT WAYNE, IN 46808

WAYNE MILLS KNITTING PARK
623 WATKINS ST, FORT WAYNE, IN 46808

UNIVERSITY OF ST FRANCIS PERFORMING ARTS CENTER
431 W BERRY ST, FORT WAYNE, IN 46802

OLD KRAUS APFELBAUM GRAIN SEED AND WOOL BUILDING
506 EDGERTON AVE, FORT WAYNE, IN 46808

THE GRAND WAYNE CONVENTION CENTER
120 W JEFFERSON BLVD, FORT WAYNE, IN 46802

J.K. O'DONNELL'S
121 W WAYNE ST, FORT WAYNE, IN 46802

THE HISTORY CENTER
302 E BERRY ST, FORT WAYNE, IN 46802

SEE THE
ARTISTIC ORIGINALS

CHECK OUT THE ARTISTIC COLOR VERSIONS
OF THESE FORT WAYNE LOCATIONS IN MY
ONLINE GALLERY

LIKE THIS BOOK?

LEAVE A REVIEW AND SHARE WITH YOUR
FRIENDS!

FOLLOW MY PHOTOGRAPHY ON
SOCIAL MEDIA

INSTAGRAM @BE.PHOTOGRAPHY.INDIANA

@BE.CREATIVE.MEDIA

FACEBOOK @BE.PHOTOGRAPHY.INDIANA

@BE.CREATIVE.MEDIA

PINTEREST BEPHOTOGRAPHYINDIANA

TIK TOK @BE.PHOTOGRAPHY.INDIANA

TWITTER @BEPHOTOGRAHYIN

YOU CAN ALSO FIND MORE PHOTO ART
POSTCARDS AND PRINTS IN MY ETSY SHOP

@OTISDESIGNBOUTIQUE.ETSY.COM

www.ingramcontent.com/pod-product-compliance
Lightning Source LLC
Chambersburg PA
CBHW080339030726
47594CB00011B/4078